For Colby —

Wooden & Me

Make today your masterpiece!

Best wishes,

[signature]

Woody Woodburn

*WOODEN & ME: Life Lessons from My Two-Decade
Friendship with the Legendary Coach and Humanitarian to Help
"Make Each Day Your Masterpiece."*
Copyright © 2013 by Woody Woodburn

First Edition, 2013
Indie Published by Woody Woodburn
woodywoodburn.com

"There is great joy in helping others."
John Wooden

Δ

For helping me with their well wishes and generous financial support in making WOODEN & ME *a reality, I hope these dear friends indeed feel great joy.*

"Manuscript" Level Patrons
Wayne and Kathy Bryan
Gene and Mary Lou Paschal
Mark and Stephenie Thomas

"Pyramid of Success" Level Patrons
Bob and Mike Bryan
Jim, Kim and John Hendrix
Dallas and Greg Woodburn

"Patrons In Print" Level Supporters
Hank and Elaine Aldrete
Jim McCoskey
John and Barbi Mensendiek
Joe and Doreen Piellucci
Ric and Penny Ruffinelli
Ed and Karen Spinardi
Laszlo and Laurie Tabori

Also by Woody Woodburn

Raising Your Child To Be A Champion In Athletics, Arts and Academics (Kensington Publishing/Citadel Press, 2004) co-written with nationally renowned speaker and coach Wayne Bryan

The Pirate Collection: A Decade of Dominance by Ventura College's Men's Basketball Team (Indie Published, 1995)

Δ

Cover design, front and back, by the extremely talented graphic artist Dianna Chrysler. A Fine Arts major at the University of Southern California, Dianna transformed the concepts by Greg Woodburn into beautiful reality. This included taking a photograph of John Wooden's actual autograph on a "Pyramid of Success" signed to Greg and turning it into the font used for the "Wooden" signature in the title. I look forward to following Dianna's bright artistic career.

Interior layout and design by Greg Woodburn.

Contents

———

For Coach –

"The journey is better than the inn" you often reminded me, and in my life journey I feel extremely thankful and blessed to have had you walking ahead of me as a role model; walking beside me as a teacher, mentor and friend; and now walking behind me in spirit as a source of continued inspiration to myself – as well as to my daughter Dallas, son Greg, and wife Lisa – for pursuing the peace of mind that is true success. Too, I am forever grateful to you Coach for the frequent reminder and constant shining example you set about *love* being the most important word in the English language.

Δ

For Lisa –

From Shakespeare: "I would not wish any companion in the world but you."

For Dallas and Greg –

I would not wish any children in the world but you.

Introduction

———

"Success is peace of mind which is a direct result
of self-satisfaction in knowing you did your best
to become the best you are capable of becoming."
— John Wooden

Δ

Reach back in your mind to the first time, probably about age four or perhaps five, when you can remember standing in line to meet Santa Claus. Likely your emotions were a medley of awe and nervousness and untethered excitement; summer butterflies dancing in a winter stomach. So it was for my great boyhood friend Brian Whalen and me as we waited our turns nearly four decades ago.

Instead of kindergarteners, however, we were fifteen-year-old junior high schoolers. Instead of December, it was July. And instead of waiting to see Saint Nick, we stood impatiently in a long, snaking line to meet The Wizard of Westwood.

It was Monday, July 28, 1975 – the first full day of the annual John Wooden Basketball Fundamentals Camp being held on the campus of Cal Lutheran University in Thousand Oaks, California. Brian and I were lined up outside the cafeteria for lunch knowing full well that Coach Wooden was personally greeting every camper at the glass double-door entrance.

Judging from the camp's group picture, Coach shook hands and shared a few kind words with about two hundred and forty kids that week. I am easy to spot in the crowded eight-by-ten black-and-white print because Brian had the wherewithal to bolt to the very back row atop the outdoor football bleachers – and I had the wherewithal to follow close behind and then stand beside him. So there I am in the top row, second from the left, standing next to Brian, who is a full head-and-one-inch taller than me.

I am now six-foot-four – about Brian's height that distant day; he went on to play varsity basketball in high school and college. But I was late maturing with a full five inches of growth coming in college, so I was maybe five-foot-nine at best that long-ago summer. During pickup games on the Balboa Junior High School blacktop basketball courts before school and at lunch breaks I would pretend to be UCLA star point guard Greg Lee throwing alley-oop lob passes to Brian, who pretended to be the Bruins' superstar center Bill Walton.

Four months prior to camp, and one hundred and forty-five miles south in San Diego, John Robert Wooden had coached the final game of his legendary career. Brian and I had watched on television as our beloved UCLA Bruins defeated the Kentucky Wildcats, 92-85, to capture their tenth – *tenth!* – NCAA national championship under Wooden's wizardly guidance. Although Wooden had held his summer basketball camp for a number of years, and Brian had attended the previous year, now we were among Coach's first "players" in his retirement.

Just as Coach Wooden did on the inaugural day of practice each season with his collegiate players, the first skill he showed us youth campers was how to put on our socks properly by smoothing out all wrinkles in order to prevent blisters. It is easy to imagine hotshot know-it-all UCLA freshmen players, much less returning All-American selections on their way to the NBA, rolling their eyes when Wooden would announce, "Gentleman, today we're going to learn how to put on our shoes and socks correctly."

Correctly meant Coach's way, which he demonstrated thusly: bunching the sock up so your toes can go all the way in to the end; next carefully inching the sock backwards onto the foot and over the heel and up the ankle; then smoothing away wrinkles from toe to heel – not heel to toe! – before lastly holding the sock taut with one hand gripped around the ankle so no wrinkles could re-

3

emerge while simultaneously using the other hand to slip the sneaker onto the foot.

"I want it done consciously, not casually," Wooden continued. "Otherwise we would not be doing everything possible to prepare in the best way."

Preparing in the best way also meant the laces should not be tied above the center of the tongue of the shoe as is conventional, but instead off to the side directly over one of the eyelets. In this way the knot was anchored and could not shift or loosen. And, of course, the tied laces should always be double-knotted. Additionally, Coach explained, sneakers should *not* have a thumb's width of space between the big toe and the end of the shoe as most everyone is always told. ("Room to grow," my dad always called this space when measuring me for new shoes.) Rather, Wooden believed, the big toe should almost be touching the inside end of the sneaker because then the foot will not slide forward – potentially causing blisters – when a player makes a jump stop. Preventing blisters, of course, is part of doing everything one can to prepare in the best way.

Indeed, Wooden went on to explain that a blister can send a player to the bench; and a benched player hurts the team. But this can all be avoided through attention to detail. Most likely during this demonstration Coach told us, "It's the little details that are vital; little things make big things happen." Too, most assuredly, he shared this familiar Wooden-ism: "Failing to prepare is preparing to fail."

I took "Shoes and Socks 101" to heart as though it were wisdom coming directly from the lips of a mountaintop guru, which it truly was since Wooden sat atop the peak of the basketball world. Ever since, for nearly four decades that have included playing basketball through my youth; competing on the intercollegiate tennis team at the University of California at Santa Barbara; running more than a dozen marathons and countless shorter road races and maintaining an active consecutive-day running streak of more than ten years; I have smoothed my socks and tied a double-knot over an eyelet and purchased my athletic shoes a half-size smaller than suggested . . . and remarkably I have never had trouble to speak of with a foot blister.

This is a lesson I taught my daughter, and in turn my son, almost as soon as each could put on their own socks and tie their own shoes. Even better, a few years later Coach Wooden gave Dallas and Greg (and me, thirty-five-momentarily-turned-fifteen once more) a refresher demonstration during an afternoon-long visit with him in his home. It was like Einstein demonstrating long division, Beethoven teaching scales.

Back to the John Wooden Basketball Fundamentals Camp. Coach, who true to his high character gave his time and effort to the camp each day rather than merely lending it his name, also taught us the fundamentals of shooting, rebounding and passing; jump stops and pivots; ball-handling and most every other aspect of the sport through his success-proven formula of "Explanation, Demonstration and Repetition, Repetition, Repetition."

Naturally, Coach gave us an inspiring lecture on his famous Pyramid of Success, a copy of which was contained inside the Player's Notebook each camper received. You can only imagine my excitement at being selected the Most Valuable Player on my team at the camp, not so much for a boost to my ego but because the award presented was a Pyramid of Success lacquered plaque. From that 1975 summer on, in my boyhood bedroom to each place I have lived since through young adulthood and marriage and middle age – college dorm rooms, apartments, condominiums and homes – that faux wood-grained Pyramid of Success has hung in a place of high honor. I can see it as I sit at my desk writing this book.

Nearby, on a wall of built-in bookshelves shoehorned tight to at least twice their intended capacity, rests a framed photograph of one of the billboards that appeared at a few locations in Torrance in the winter of 2002 featuring me posed with a tennis racket, golf club and hockey stick while holding a football in my passing hand and spinning a basketball on my left index finger. The slogan reads: *"Columnist Woody Woodburn: He Writes. He Scores. South Bay's Best."* Because I was commuting sixty miles from Ventura, no one in my family saw the billboards. Or, for that matter, even knew about them.

That changed about a month after the billboards first went up when my newspaper editor mailed me the framed color photo as a keepsake. Lisa, Dallas and Greg were mildly upset I had not told them about the heady public advertisement.

"You never asked me if I was on a billboard," I replied in jest.

Truth is, I honestly never thought of coming home and announcing, "Guess what? I'm on a billboard!" After all, as Coach advised, "Talent is God given. Be humble. Fame is man-given. Be grateful. Conceit is self-given. Be careful." Also, I grew up with two older brothers who made sure I knew the dangers of getting an inflated ego by personally popping my bubble when necessary.

On this same bookshelf I still have my Player's Notebook from camp. Forty-eight photocopied black-and-white pages staple-bound in a white cardstock cover with blue printing, the simple notebook features far more than basketball fundamentals and diagramed plays of the famous UCLA High Post Options. It also contains life lessons, and it is these pages that have been dog-eared and show the wear of being read time and again.

To be sure, I devoured the "General Comments and Philosophy of Coach Wooden" that include:

> *Be a gentleman at all times.*
> *Be a team player always.*
> *Be on time whenever time is involved.*
> *Never criticize, nag or razz a teammate.*
> *Never expect favors.*
> *Never be selfish, jealous, envious, or egotistical.*
> *Never alibi or make excuses.*
> *Politeness is a small price to pay to get the*
>   *goodwill and affection of others. It will*
>   *reap many benefits in the end.*

And, in all capital letters, this classic Wooden-ism: *THE PLAYER WHO GIVES HIS BEST IS SURE OF SUCCESS, WHILE THE PLAYER WHO GIVES LESS THAN HIS BEST IS A FAILURE.* It goes without saying that "PLAYER" could well be changed to "PERSON" and the dictum would be equally true.

My junior high school English teachers had failed to raise poetry above drudgery, but Coach Wooden – a former English teacher who always considered himself a teacher rather than a coach – sparked my interest with his inclusion of a selection of his favorite poems in the Player's Notebook. These include "The Great Competitor" by the legendary sportswriter Grantland Rice, a poem that, among numerous others, Coach would many years later recite on our walks together and visits in his home:

> *Beyond the winning and the goal,*
> *Beyond the glory and the fame,*
> *He feels a flame within his soul,*
> *Born of the spirit of the game.*
>
> *And where the barriers may wait,*
> *Built by the opposing gods,*
> *He finds a thrill in bucking fate*
> *And riding down the endless odds.*
>
> *Where others wither in the fire,*
> *Or fall below some raw mishap,*
> *Where others lag behind and tire,*
> *Or break beneath the handicap,*
>
> *He finds a new and deeper thrill*
> *To take him on the uphill spin,*
> *Because the test is greater still*
> *And something he can revel in.*

Another poem featured in the Player's Notebook is "Are You A Winner Or A Loser?" by Sidney Harris. During afternoon rest breaks and before lights-out in our shared Cal Lutheran University dorm room, Brian and I worked to memorize its entirety over the course of our week at camp because we wanted to be winners:

A winner says, "Let's find out;" A loser says, "Nobody knows."

When a winner makes a mistake, he says, "I was wrong;" when a loser makes a mistake, he says, It wasn't my fault."

A winner credits his "good luck" for winning — even though it isn't good luck; a loser blames his "bad luck" for losing — even though it isn't bad luck.

A winner knows how and when to say "Yes" and "No"; a loser says, "Yes, but" and "perhaps not" at the wrong time, for the wrong reasons.

A winner isn't nearly as afraid of losing as a loser is secretly afraid of winning.

A winner works harder than a loser and has more time; a loser is always "too busy" to do what is necessary.

A winner goes through a problem; a loser goes around it and never gets past it.

A winner makes commitments; a loser makes promises.

A winner shows he's sorry by making up for it; a loser says "I'm sorry," but does the same thing next time.

A winner says, "I'm good, but not as good as I ought to be"; a loser says, "I'm not as bad as a lot of other people."

A winner listens; A loser just waits until it's his turn to talk.

A winner would rather be admired than liked, although he would prefer both; a loser would rather be liked than admired and is even willing to pay the price of mild contempt for it.

> *A winner respects those who are superior to*
> *him and tries to learn something from*
> *them; a loser resents those who are*
> *superior to him and tries to find*
> *chinks in their armour.*
> *A winner says, "There ought to be a better way*
> *to do it"; a loser says, "That's the way*
> *it's always been done here."*

To which Wooden added: "If you look like a winner, you feel like a winner; if you feel like a winner, you act like a winner; if you act like a winner, you play like a winner."

The final page of the Player's Notebook is an unattributed poem titled "Press On" which, I have since learned, is actually the first five stanzas of a piece authored by Calvin Coolidge titled "Persistence":

> *Nothing in the world*
> *can take the place of persistence.*
>
> *Talent will not;*
> *nothing is more common than*
> *unsuccessful men with talent.*
>
> *Genius will not;*
> *unrewarded genius is almost a proverb.*
>
> *Education will not;*
> *the world is full of educated derelicts.*
>
> *Persistence and determination*
> *alone are omnipotent.*

(The title in the Player's Notebook version of the poem comes from a stanza not included: *"The slogan 'PRESS ON' has solved and always will solve the problems of the human race."*)

Δ

Attending the John Wooden Basketball Fundamentals Camp is a cherished memory that belongs in the red velvet-lined heirloom box of my mind's eye, but I would be lying if I were to say that the week taught me how to truly be "A Great Competitor" and a "Winner" who will always "Press On." Age fifteen is probably too young to absorb these life lessons fully, or even in a strong dose; at least for me such was the case.

And yet, as the Buddhist proverb states, "When the student is ready, the teacher will appear." Twelve years after my experience at The John Wooden Basketball Fundamentals Camp, I was ready and the teacher re-appeared. Now the year was 1987 and I was a young sportswriter at a small-town daily newspaper, with big professional dreams. Now I was married to my college sweetheart with our first child on the way. Now the curriculum would be "Life" Fundamentals and the "Camp" would last not six days but instead span twenty-three years. Now, as then, the teacher would be Coach John Robert Wooden.

In his wonderful novel *A River Runs Through It*, Norman Maclean writes that "stories of life are often more like rivers than books." The currents of my life had brought me back to Coach. I had no way of realizing it at the moment, but my personal story would be forever changed positively, profoundly, perpetually. In every facet, from husband and parent and son to writer and friend and citizen, I was to become better. Assuredly, just as with each and every individual who played on his high school and college basketball teams, Coach Wooden wanted me to be a good person in all aspects of my life. He wanted me to be successful by his definition – *doing your best to become the best you are capable of becoming* – not necessarily by society's metrics of salary and status and power and possessions.

To be certain, Coach never equated money with success. For example, when I asked if he ever considered leaving UCLA to coach in the NBA, he shared that in the late nineteen-sixties he was contacted by a number of professional teams including Jack Kent Cooke, who then owned the Los Angeles Lakers.

"Were you tempted?" I asked Coach.

"Never."

"But surely you were offered a lot of money?"

With a twinkle in his eye: "Oh, my, yes."

"So weren't you tempted, even a little?"

Without hesitation: "Never," he repeated.

Nor did Coach use the lucrative offers from the pros as leverage to negotiate a better deal from UCLA, where his highest annual salary was an astonishingly low $37,500.

A number of years ago I was approached to ghostwrite a book and also asked what my requested fee would be. Negotiating is something I have little talent or fondness for. Coach offered me wonderful counsel, explaining that he avoided the back-and-forth Ping-Pong of negotiating for his public speaking fees by simply telling an interested party upfront to make its *first* offer its very *best* offer, because he would not come back with a counteroffer nor give them a chance to make a second offer. He would either accept or decline the initial proposal. Period. Coach said he found this process to work well; I now agree. Perhaps competitive negotiation would result in higher paydays, but in my experience the simplicity and peace of mind afforded by doing it Coach Wooden's way yields a reward that exceeds any diminished financial returns.

It was actually the second time Coach had come through for me on a book project. In 2004, I co-authored the parenting book *Raising Your Child to be a Champion in Athletics, Arts and Academics* with Wayne Bryan, a nationally renowned speaker and tennis coach as well as the father of identical twins Mike and Bob, who are the winningest doubles team in tennis history. Wayne is also a longtime mentor of mine whose Wooden-like wisdom includes, "If you don't make an effort to help those who are less fortunate than you are, then you're just wasting your life" and "Don't tell me about your dreams of a castle, show me the stones you laid today." Coach Wooden kindly read a preview copy of our book and wrote a blurb for the cover: *Since "parenting" is the most important profession for the future welfare of all mankind, I urge all to read "Raising Your Child to be a Champion."* It was a priceless endorsement.

Priceless is how I feel about a stack of letters from Coach, mailed to me at five different addresses through my adult life, that I keep in a small fireproof safe along with other pen-and-paper family heirlooms and important documents. I similarly cherish a leather basketball given to me as a gift when I turned thirty-three signed in perfect schoolteacher's script and: "*Happy Birthday, Woody, and best wishes for many more. Love, John Wooden 5/27/93.*"

However, even more dear to me than any memorabilia gem or similarly personalized autographed gifts that include a framed Pyramid of Success and a UCLA jersey, are the handful of treasured photos on display throughout my home. They include:

A five-by-seven-inch grainy black-and-white print of Coach and me snapped by a photographer colleague from my newspaper after I interviewed Wooden for the first time twenty-six years ago when he gave a motivational speech to a local business group. Leaning in towards each another, Coach is wearing a sport coat and tie and wide smile and I am wearing a collared shirt and dark sweater and wider smile. To give you some measure of how precious this picture is to me, I have on display only two other framed photographs of famous people I have met during my career: sharing a moment with my writing idol Jim Murray, and shaking hands with former President Ronald Reagan in the Los Angeles Dodgers clubhouse.

Coach and me again, again five-by-seven-inches, about a decade later, this time in color. I like this snapshot even more than the first because it is more intimate and reveals our growing friendship that has been irrigated by visits and phone calls and letters. Coach, wearing a pale blue dress shirt with the top button open, has his right arm wrapped around my waist. His smile this time is a little smaller, but also more genuine with more warmth. When I look at this picture I see myself not posed with a famous figure, but rather sharing a private moment with a grandfather figure.

Dearer still is the eight-by-ten-inch color photo of Dallas, then ten years old, and Greg, then seven, sitting on Coach's lap in his study when they spent a magical afternoon with him sixteen summers past. Coach, beaming, has his left arm around Dallas, who is dressed up for the occasion in her favorite sunflower-print dress and a bright yellow headband to match; the two are also holding hands. Meanwhile, Coach embraces Greg with his right arm. Not only are the two smiling children sitting on his lap, but Coach is gently, lovingly, pulling them both in closer towards him like a great-grandfather enjoying a visit with his "Little Ones" – that being the term of endearment Coach often used when referring to his own great-grandchildren. Similarly, about Dallas and Greg he would invariably ask me: "How are the Little Ones?"

As a writer I am asked from time to time to be a guest speaker at civic groups and service clubs, and the person the audiences consistently want to hear more about during the Q&A afterwards is John Wooden. This works out nicely because I most enjoy talking about him. In fact, during my twenty-five-plus years as a sports columnist (and now general interest columnist) I have written more pieces on Coach than any other individual, and by a solid margin. For many years, readers of my columns and listeners at my guest talks have encouraged me to write a book about my experiences and friendship with Coach Wooden.

At long last I have heeded that sage advice. Coach helped shape my life, and grandly. My friendship-menteeship with him is a precious gift, one that came wrapped with a bow of responsibility to share with others the life lessons he shared with me. I have come to realize it is not enough that I have raised my twenty-six-year-old daughter and twenty-three-year-old son to be John Wooden disciples who speak and think and act in Wooden-isms. Dallas and Greg both even have one of Coach's favorite aphorisms on their smartphone wallpaper: "Make each day your masterpiece." Lisa, my dear wife of thirty-one years, and I also have this same reminder of enlightenment on our phone screens. Were I to ever get a tattoo – which Coach would have strongly frowned upon – I would choose those five words: "Make each day your masterpiece" beneath a fifteen-block Pyramid of Success.

Coach passed away on June 4, 2010, just four months shy of his 100th birthday. Even when he was still alive it was impossible for me to repay him for the great kindnesses he extended to me, and my family, over the span of nearly a quarter-century. Instead, the best I can strive for is to pay forward his generosity in some small measure by sharing his wisdom and life lessons with others who were not similarly blessed to know him, visit with him, walk with him. My desire is to extend the kindness he showed me by extending the reach of his "classroom." It is my hope that through the pages of *Wooden & Me* you, too, will be inspired to "Make Each Day Your Masterpiece."

One

The Talk

"Listen if you want to be heard."
— *John Wooden*

Δ

Time can be a silent thief, and nearly forty years after my great boyhood friend Brian Whalen and I went to summer basketball camp together I cannot precisely recall what Coach John Wooden said to me when it was my turn to shake his hand at the Cal Lutheran University cafeteria entrance that first full day. Most likely Coach greeted me with a warm hello and maybe sincerely asked how my morning had gone; possibly he reminded me to tuck my T-shirt into my basketball shorts or perhaps inspected my shoelaces to make sure they were pulled snug and double-knotted over an eyelet.

Although the exact words he spoke to me that day are lost to time, in all the years since I have never forgotten this: the moment was magical and it mattered. I had met The Wizard of Westwood.

Flash forward a dozen years later to another momentous moment; to Thursday, February 19, 1987. I was now twenty-six years old and the sports editor/writer/columnist for the Santa Maria Times in Central California. It was my third newspaper in four years – after stops in the high desert at Twentynine Palms and then in Paso Robles on the Central Coast – and the largest thus far with a circulation of about 30,000. On this day John Wooden was the keynote speaker at a corporate luncheon in San Luis Obispo and I was there to write a column about him.

Dressed nattily in gray slacks, navy blue sport coat, white dress shirt and a perfectly knotted red-and-blue striped tie, his full head of silver hair neatly parted high on the left side, the seventy-six-year-old Wooden spoke extemporaneously for a full forty minutes, the whole while enchanting the audience of three-hundred businesspeople with witty stories and professorial wisdom. At times during his talk he seemed like Poor Richard's Almanac in the flesh as he shared such Wooden-isms as "Failure to prepare is preparing to fail"; "Be quick but don't hurry"; and "Be at your best when your best is needed."

Also, as you would expect, Wooden spent a fair share of time talking about basketball, noting for instance to the rapt audience: "Winning with Lewis Alcindor" – Coach, out of habit and not stubbornness or disrespect, still referred to Kareem Abdul-Jabbar by his former name from his UCLA playing days – "was not my greatest joy. It was expected. Nineteen-sixty-four was wonderful. We weren't even listed in the top-fifty before the season began."

That 1964 team, with no starter taller than six-foot-five, went undefeated en route to cutting down the nets for Wooden's first NCAA championship as a coach. His UCLA Bruin teams would go on to win nine more national titles for an unparalleled tally of ten championships over a twelve-year span, seven of them coming consecutively. It was a Gettysburg Address-like achievement for greatness in brevity. Moreover, the mindboggling feats also included a record eighty-eight-game winning streak along the way; thirty-eight straight victories in the NCAA Tournament; and four perfect seasons.

All this winning, and yet John Wooden told the audience that afternoon: "I never used the word 'win.' If we played our best, who scored the most points wasn't important." After a perfectly timed two-beat pause, Coach added with a mischievous grin: "Of course, if we played our best the final score was usually to our liking."

Indeed. Wooden's coaching career won-loss record was 885-203 and in twenty-nine years his college teams never had a losing season. The surprise is that he was named college Coach of the Year *only* five times. He was also deservedly named "Coach of the Century" for all sports, amateur or professional, by *The Sporting News* in 2000. Too, he was the first person enshrined into Basketball Hall of Fame both as a player (1960) and coach (1972). James Naismith may have invented the sport, but John Wooden came closest to perfecting it.

All this basketball greatness and fame, and yet the bulk of Wooden's talk in San Luis Obispo focused on his Pyramid of Success. He shared that in 1934, as a young high school English teacher, he was unhappy with the familiar A-B-C grading system. For a gifted student a "B" might not be the best he or she could do, Wooden explained, while for another student earning a "C" might indicate true accomplishment.

Further inspired by a poem, which he recited to the audience – *At God's footstool, to confess, / A poor soul knelt and bowed his head. / "I failed," he cried. The master said, / "Thou didst thy best. That is success."* – Coach decided to come up with his own definition of *success* and settled on this: "Success is peace of mind which is the direct result of self-satisfaction in knowing you did your best to become the best you are capable of becoming."

Additionally, the then-young Wooden began erecting his now-famous Pyramid of Success. He completed it *fourteen* years later – only six years less than required to erect the Great Pyramid of Giza. But, as the mortar securing the pinnacle of the final structure extols and as Wooden's initial sixteen seasons at UCLA's helm before achieving his first NCAA championship exemplifies: "Patience – Good things take time."

More than once Coach would elaborate in person with me over the ensuing two decades: "Remember, Woody, good things take time – and good things should take time. Usually *a lot* of time." It is a valuable lesson I have leaned on many times and one that my son once poetically rephrased to Coach's visible pleasure: "Patience is a bitter seed that bears sweet fruit."

The two cornerstones of the Pyramid of Success, Wooden lectured to the adults at the corporate luncheon in San Luis Obispo just as he had to us kids at basketball camp in Thousand Oaks, are Industriousness ("There is no substitute for work. Worthwhile things come from hard work and careful planning") and Enthusiasm ("Your heart must be in your work").

The three remaining stones on the bottom row are:

Friendship – "Comes from mutual esteem, respect and devotion. Like marriage it must not be taken for granted but requires joint effort."

Loyalty – "To yourself and to all those depending upon you. Keep your self-respect."

Cooperation – "With all levels of your co-workers. Listen if you want to be heard. Be interested in finding the best way, not in having your own way."

Moving up to the second row:

Self-Control – "Practice self-discipline and keep emotions under control. Good judgment and common sense are essential."

Alertness – "Be observing constantly. Stay open-minded. Be eager to learn and improve."

Initiative – "Cultivate the ability to make decisions and think alone. Do not be afraid of failure, but learn from it."

Intentness – "Set a realistic goal. Concentrate on its achievement by resisting all temptations and being determined and persistent."

The three blocks at the heart of the Pyramid are:

Condition – "Mental, Moral, Physical. Rest, exercise, and diet must be considered. Moderation must be practiced. Dissipation must be eliminated."

Skill – "A knowledge of and the ability to properly and quickly execute the fundamentals. Be prepared and cover every little detail."

Team Spirit – "A genuine consideration for others. An eagerness to sacrifice personal interests or glory for the welfare of all."

The two penultimate blocks:

Poise – "Just being yourself. Being at ease in any situation. Never fighting yourself."

Confidence – "Respect without fear. May come from being prepared and keeping all things in proper perspective."

And resting alone atop of the Pyramid of Success: Competitive Greatness – "Be at your best when your best is needed. Enjoyment of a difficult challenge."

Holding these fifteen building blocks securely in place is the vital mortar whose recipe is a mix of Ambition, Sincerity, Adaptability, Honesty, Resourcefulness, Reliability, Fight, Integrity, Faith and Patience. In other words, the Pyramid's enduring strength comes from Wooden's rock-solid Midwestern values.

One of myriad examples of Wooden's iron character is how he reacted to the loss of his hard-earned life savings on the eve of his marriage to Nellie Riley on Sunday, August 8, 1932. The morning prior the happy ceremony, Coach went to the bank to withdraw a portion of his savings to pay for the wedding as well as to buy a new Plymouth he had ordered. But the bank was closed – for good, another Great Depression casualty. Gone, to the final nickel, was Wooden's $909.05 savings; no small sum in 1932.

It was a heartbreaking turn of events and while he felt terrible for Nellie and himself, Wooden felt worse for the many elderly people who had similarly lost their money. As he wrote forty years later in *They Call Me Coach*: "We were young and could bounce back." That they did, making the best of the way things turned out by borrowing two-hundred dollars and getting married as planned – and then spending their first week apart as newlyweds while Coach earned a much-needed twenty-five dollars helping teach an out-of-town basketball clinic. Certainly not the ideal honeymoon, and yet, just as a hotter fire produces a harder steel, perhaps this early challenge – and the Competitive Greatness to successfully be at their best when their best was needed – helped forge their long unbreakable relationship.

An incident from Wooden's first college coaching job and his unexpected journey to UCLA offers further lessons in living authentically by one's core principles. After completing his World War II military service in 1946, Wooden was hired at Indiana State Teachers' College (presently known as Indiana State University). In his first season he led the Sycamores to the conference title. Along with the banner, the team received a berth in the prestigious the National Association of Intercollegiate Athletics (NAIA) Tournament.

However, because African-American players were forbidden to participate in the tournament, Wooden personally rejected the invitation. Clarence Walker played very few minutes for the Sycamores so his absence would surely have had little impact on the team's chances, but Coach still would not consider participating without him. It was another example of John Wooden showing in deed that our conscience must be our North Star.

After guiding the Sycamores to another conference championship the following season, and a runner-up finish in the NAIA Tournament that had now reversed its discriminatory policy, Wooden was courted by both Minnesota and UCLA in 1948. Minnesota held an edge because Coach dreamed of returning to his Big Ten roots. Minnesota needed final approval from its Board before presenting an official offer, so its athletic director agreed to call Wooden at 6 p.m.; Wooden further arranged for UCLA – his second choice – to phone an hour later, by which time Coach would know Minnesota's decision.

Six o'clock came and went without a phone call from Minnesota. When UCLA rang at 7 p.m. sharp and made its offer, Wooden accepted.

But hold the phone! At about eight o'clock that night Minnesota's A.D. finally called – he had been delayed from doing so at the appointed time because of a severe snowstorm. In light of this, few would have blamed Wooden for changing his mind. After all, he had verbally accepted UCLA's offer less than an hour earlier and there had not yet even been time to send out a press release. Nor had a contract been signed. Surely Wooden could have phoned UCLA, explained the situation to the Bruins' athletic director and apologetically withdrawn his acceptance in order to go with his top choice. In fact, this is what Minnesota's A.D. asked him to do.

Wooden, however, stood strong as a mighty oak in a howling snowstorm. He did not waver. He had given his word and his word was his bond. While one can easily imagine Wooden would have accomplished great, great things coaching in the Big Ten at Minnesota, it is hard to argue that things did not turn out for the best for him because he made the best of the way the snowstorm turned out.

Wooden's handling of the UCLA and Minnesota offers gave me particular guidance about twenty years ago when a newspaper near Philadelphia flew me out to interview for an opening as its lead sports columnist. It would be a big step forward in my career at a larger-circulation paper in a terrific (pronounced "rabid") sports city and, not unimportantly, it would come with a salary increase that would make it possible for Lisa and me to buy our first home.

The interview went exceedingly well and while driving me to the airport to fly home on a Friday afternoon, the managing editor told me privately he was certain the job would be mine although he could not officially offer it to me yet because his committee had scheduled a few more candidates to interview on Monday. As he shook my hand goodbye he promised to call me the following Tuesday.

Tuesday came and went and so did Wednesday. When the managing editor finally phoned Thursday he apologized for the delay, explaining one of the remaining interviews had been pushed back, and then enthusiastically offered me the position as he had predicted he would. I wanted to accept on the spot but felt I should first tell my editor in Ventura where I had worked for six years. Naively I was not seeking a counter offer, but that is exactly what happened – not monetarily, but a promise to have more opportunities to cover big-time events in Los Angeles. I was suddenly glad I had not made a commitment to Philly just yet.

Upon further consideration and discussion with Lisa, we felt that while a bigger paycheck would be welcomed and I would personally love the professional challenge and excitement of moving to Philadelphia, it would be best for our young kids to remain in Ventura where they had begun elementary school and made some great friends; lived less than two miles from their paternal grandfather they loved dearly and saw often; had a handful of cousins nearby; and were within driving distance of their beloved maternal grandparents and extended family in Northern California.

When I called the Philly editor back, he immediately upped his monetary offer – and substantially – but I declined, expressing my gratitude but explaining I had decided to remain in Ventura for family reasons. He graciously understood and kindly suggested that I should use his new offer as leverage to sweeten my deal for staying at my newspaper. I thanked him for his counsel, but did not follow it because I had already given my word to my current editor. I may have lost out on a potential raise, but I maintained the integrity of my word and was true to myself.

Wooden's inner character was further revealed during the Question-and-Answer session that followed his keynote talk in San Luis Obispo when he was asked by an audience member, "What was the biggest highlight of your career?"

"When Nellie married me," Coach answered, without so much as a hiccup's hesitation for thought. "My children, grandchildren and great-grandchildren are the highlights of my career. They are more meaningful than any game."

With the mention of Nellie, the heartbreak of her death twenty-three months prior remained fresh in Coach's voice. They were high school sweethearts and had been married fifty-three years when she died on March 21, 1985, after a courageous battle with cancer. In the years to come

Coach would tell me more about Nellie, and gradually the memories of "the only girl I ever dated" came in a happier tone, although an ether of sadness never fully dissipated.

Following his motivational message, Wooden warmly shook hands and politely posed for snapshots and signed autographs until the very last audience member had been most charmingly accommodated. Meanwhile, I waited off in the wings to request a one-on-one interview for my column. Despite facing a three-hour drive home to Encino, Coach courteously made time for me – more than half an hour, in fact. Before asking my first question, I shyly shared, "I went to your camp at Cal Lutheran in 1975."

Smiling instantly, Wooden replied enthusiastically: "Why, yes, I remember you!" This was obviously far from true, yet it was typical of Wooden's warmth and quick charm.

When my column bearing the headline "Homespun Hoosier is a Wizard" ran in *The Santa Maria Times* I clipped the piece out and mailed it to Coach, thanking him for his time and the pleasant interview. To my great surprise a letter arrived a few days later with a *Mr. & Mrs. John Wooden* return address label on it. Inside, on his personal stationary – *From the Desk of John Wooden* – in perfect cursive as elegant as he, it read:

3-14-87

Dear Woody,

Your words of commendation were very kind and deeply appreciated as was your article regarding my presentation in San Luis Obispo.

Although it is often used without true feeling, when it is used with sincerity, no collection of words can be more expressive or meaningful than the very simple word – Thanks!

Sincerely,
John Wooden

As if this were not thrill enough, there was a postscript that made my heart accelerate like the glory-day Bruins' full-court press in action – he invited me to join him on his morning walk sometime when I was in the Encino area and included his home phone number. I could not believe my great fortune. I reread the letter several times, like someone checking and double-checking the numbers on a winning lottery ticket.

As nervous as a middle schooler phoning a girl for a first date, I rehearsed what I was going to say and then called Coach that very evening before he could forget who the heck I was. We set the date for March 31, a Tuesday, a day so special I marked it down in my calendar book of birthdays and anniversary dates to always remember.

Two

The Walk

———

"Be quick, but don't hurry."
— John Wooden

Δ

For the next two weeks I was my old boyhood self impatiently counting down the days until my birthday. At long last The Big Day arrived. Coach had told me to arrive 7 a.m. so I laid out my clothes and running shoes the night before, set my alarm for 4 a.m. and left home shortly thereafter for the one-hundred-and-thirty-mile drive from Santa Maria to Encino because I wanted to take no chances on being late. As Wooden noted in my basketball camp Player's Notebook: "Be on time whenever time is involved."

I exited the Southbound 101 Freeway at White Oak Avenue, turned right at the end of the off-ramp and then right again one block later, and quickly arrived at Coach's residence. I was a full half-hour early and nervously sat in my car waiting for the appointed meeting time to finally arrive. At seven o'clock sharp I pressed the buzzer outside the condominium's entrance and Coach, true to his code, was ready and waiting and immediately came out.

After warm pleasantries on a cool and dewy Southern California spring morning we set forth. For decades Coach had walked five miles daily, but he explained he had recently shortened his favorite route through his neighborhood to four and half miles. Despite this minor concession to Father Time, at age seventy-six Coach still moved at a surprisingly quick – but unhurried – clip.

Our walk began with me asking basketball question after basketball question. Mostly, Coach talked and I listened intently. He answered my queries about his great teams and star players and most memorable games, but gradually the conversation veered to other topics. At one street corner, as we waited for a traffic light to change from red to green, my new walking companion told me he had once received a jaywalking ticket as this very intersection. Coach sheepishly admitted he had indeed technically been guilty of the infraction because he had stepped down off the curb to wait at street level an instant before the "DON'T WALK" sign changed to "WALK."

While accepting blame and noting he had failed to follow his own advice to "Be quick, but don't hurry," Coach also felt the police officer could have shown better judgment. He compared it to a basketball official calling a lane violation on a player who has lined up with his toe barely touching the line – an infraction, yes, but a minor one made with no intention of trying to gain an advantage, and in fact none acquired. This observation surprised me because I would have assumed Coach Wooden – "St. John" who the great sports columnist Jim Murray once memorably wrote was "so square he is divisible by four" – would be a stickler to the letter of the rulebook in basketball. And yet Coach's viewpoint on both matters made great sense.

It was a lesson I have called upon often since, looking at the intent of others rather than focusing solely on their actions. Is the sales clerk ignoring me, or is she simply overwhelmed with other customers and duties? Did that driver rudely cut me off on purpose, or perhaps not see me in his blind spot? Is a waiter's intent to provide slow service, or more likely is he covering an extra table or two and the kitchen staff has fallen behind as well?

As we neared the end of our walking circuit back to his front door, Coach stopped to buy a newspaper from a newsrack. This morning it was *USA Today,* but sometimes he would choose *The Los Angeles Times* and other days *The L.A. Daily News.* Without breaking stride he rolled it up quickly and tightly – and, I am certain, unconsciously – into a baton. I could not help but smile as it reminded me of Wooden's trademark coaching ritual of rolling up the game program right before every tipoff and holding it like that for the entire contest. To my nostalgic eyes, it was like when I interviewed a long-retired Muhammad Ali and out of the blue he threw a couple of lightening-quick shadow-boxing punches in the air. A wonderful time-machine moment.

I had never yet met a queen or king or president, but after that morning I figured doing so would pale in comparison to walking with The Wizard of Westwood. I was right, at least on the latter point; a few years later I briefly met Ronald Reagan in the Los Angeles Dodgers' clubhouse before a game and while it was truly a goose-bumps thrill to meet a former American president, it ranked well below my visits with Coach.

On our first walk together I asked Coach if he missed coaching. "No, not the games or NCAA Tournaments, anyway," he answered. "But I do miss the practices. I enjoyed being with the boys every day."

We talked about some of his "boys," all middle-aged men or older now; about Gail Goodrich, who responded best to soft pats on the back in encouragement and about Walt Hazzard, who needed a "firmer pat, a little lower down"; about Kareem Abdul-Jabbar, who Coach still affectionately referred to as "Lewis" and about Jamaal Wilkes whom Coach similarly still called "Keith" even though, like Abdul-Jabbar, he had long since changed his name for religious reasons; about Bill Walton and on and on, a constellation of bright stars in the basketball sky.

Near the end of our walk we stopped for breakfast at McDonald's. Had I joined Coach the previous morning, or the following day, we would have grabbed breakfast at a nearby doughnut shop because he alternated between the two spots. At the doughnut shop he told me he always ordered a plain "old-fashioned" which struck me as absolutely perfect. This day at McDonald's he ordered scrambled eggs, sausage and coffee; I got the same except with orange juice; and despite my protestations Coach insisted on paying.

A few years later VIPs Café, less than a mile and a half from Wooden's home, became his spot of choice almost seven days a week. Coach even had his own reserved booth – officially "Table No. 2" to the wait staff – where he would sit each morning reading the newspaper and talking with other regular patrons. I think he especially liked VIPs because he was rarely asked for autographs there, though of course when he was he always graciously obliged. In a tribute as wonderful in its own way as any since his passing, Table No. 2 now bears a memorial plaque inscribed *Reserved: Coach John Wooden's Favorite Booth.*

After we took our trays and were seated at a table in McDonald's, Coach bowed his head even for this simple fastfood meal and silently prayed before eating. Although I typically had only done so at Thanksgiving and Christmas dinners, I followed his lead.

His quiet display of faith reminded me about having read that Coach always carried a silver cross with him and I asked if I could see it. He happily showed me, explaining it was a gift from his minister before Wooden went into the Navy in 1942; he pointed out how its edges were worn smooth after decades of being rubbed between his thumb and fingers. From memory Coach then recited a poem by Verna Thomas McGehee, a copy of which he later mailed to me:

The Cross In My Pocket

I carry a cross in my pocket,
a simple reminder to me
of the fact that I am a Christian
wherever I may be;

This little cross is not magic,
nor is it a good-luck charm,
It isn't meant to protect me
from every physical harm;

It's not for identification
for all the world to see,
It's simply an understanding
between my Savior and me;

When I put my hand in my pocket
to bring out a coin or key,
The cross is there to remind me
of the price He paid for me;

It reminds me, too, to be thankful
for my blessings day by day,
and to strive to serve Him better
in all that I do and say;

It is also a daily reminder of
the peace and comfort I share
with all who know my Master
and give themselves to His care;

So I carry a cross in my pocket
reminding me, no one but me,
that Jesus Christ is the Lord of my life
if only I will let Him be.

When my two older brothers, young sister and I were very young my parents took us to church with some regularity. But as we grew older and youth football and basketball leagues and tennis tournaments began to fill up our weekends, our attendance gradually diminished although Jim and Doug did go through Confirmation. We stopped going altogether after we moved from Ohio to California in June of 1972 when I was twelve – Jim was seventeen; Doug, fifteen; and Kim, nine – because my mom could not find a minister in town that she wholeheartedly liked.

While I did not begin attending church again following my first breakfast with Coach, seeing him clasp his hands together, close his eyes and bow his head in silent prayer reawakened a spiritualness within me. I started giving thanks in my mind at each meal. Later, Lisa and I began asking Dallas and Greg to each share a thought of gratitude at the family dinner table, a tradition that continues to this day.

Coach's deep faith gave me strength, and perhaps more importantly provided my father with a sense of comfort (as I will share in more detail later), in 1992 when my mom died without warning of a massive heart attack at age sixty.

It was during our first breakfast together, and later when we returned to Coach's condominium to extend our visit another hour, that our conversation grew more intimate. He talked about Nell a great deal. I sensed, as I later would with my dad when he was in the similar situation, that for Coach sharing memories about his late wife was painful, yes, but also somehow therapeutic and comforting.

I was honored to listen as he told me about Nell being "my only sweetheart" and about catching her eye in the stands and giving her a wink right before the tipoff of every game he coached. In his study he pointed out the ten NCAA championship plaques on the wall and proudly explained that it had been Nell's idea to arrange them from bottom row to top – four, three, two, one – in a pyramid.

Coach also told me about his children, grandchildren and first great-grandchild, Cori. Coach said that babysitting Cori, then just a toddler, could really wear him out. But it was obvious he delighted in chasing after her. In fact, he credited Cori – who was born not long after Nell passed away – with eventually pulling him out of a deep depression by giving his life a new sense of purpose.

Coach asked me about my writing and my life and was delighted to learn I was going to become a father in August. He asked when Lisa's due date was and when I replied August 8, his eyes misted up instantly and visibly. August 8, he shared, was his and Nell's wedding anniversary; the coming one would have been their fifty-fifth. That figure put me in awe; I had been married a mere four years.

I was two months from turning twenty-seven; Coach was then seventy-six – the exact age at which my paternal grandfather died when I was seven. I did not realize this coincidence until later, but it did strike me right away sitting in Coach's living room that I felt like I was not with a living legend so much as visiting with what I remembered my grandfather to be like. To this day my father calls his dad "the greatest man I ever knew."

Like Wooden, my Grandpa Ansel was raised on a

Midwestern farm – in Ohio rather than Indiana. Like Wooden, Grandpa enjoyed literature greatly, especially Shakespeare and particularly *Hamlet*. Like Wooden, Grandpa loved poetry and wrote some verse.

And like Wooden, Grandpa had once been a schoolteacher, albeit for only a few years in order to earn tuition for medical school. Dr. Ansel Woodburn returned to his small hometown of Urbana and enjoyed a long career as a country physician, often receiving payment in the form of a chicken or eggs or produce during the Great Depression and just as frequently providing free care. Because of this, it took Ansel more than thirty years to repay his medical school tuition debts.

A passage in Norman Maclean's wonderful novel *A River Runs Through It* seems as though it was written with Ansel in mind:

> He was a small-town doctor, and I have never asked a big-town doctor for his opinion of the small-town doctor's medical examination. I am sure, though, that no big-town doctor ever said what the small-town doctor said to me next. He said: "You come see me late tomorrow morning in my office, do you hear? If you don't come tomorrow, I'll charge you for tonight. If you come tomorrow, I won't charge you for tomorrow or tonight. All I want is to know that you are well."

So esteemed was Grandpa Ansel, with his wellspring of kindness and good humor alloyed with iron morals and an unbendable work ethic, that numerous boy babies he delivered were named in his honor. Indeed, I have seen circa World War II editions of *The Urbana Citizen* daily newspaper with stories and photographs of numerous local young servicemen and boys with the first or middle name of Ansel. Now as then: my son's middle name is Ansel.

Grandpa's familiar reminder to my big brothers and me, "If something's worth doing, it's worth doing right," surely echoed Coach's oft-repeated aphorism, "If you don't have time to do it right, when will you have time to do it over?" Similarly, Grandpa's "If you don't learn anything today it will be a wasted day" dovetailed perfectly with Coach's "Learn as if you were to live forever; live as if you were to die tomorrow."

Stored securely in my small fireproof steel box with less important documents like our mortgage papers, automobile pink slips and some savings bonds, I have a handful of Grandpa's letters (along with my letters from Wooden); a couple pages containing random musings and observations Ansel jotted down, like, "The only way to travel life's road is to cross one bridge at a time" and "Re: Physical handicaps – I play the saxophone because my arms are too short for the trombone" and "It is good at times to deal with ignorant people because it makes you feel so smart." Also within is this poem he handwrote inside the eighth edition of the book "Modern Surgery" dated October 1919:

The worker dies, but the work lives on
Whether a picture, a book, or a clock
Ticking the minutes of life away
For another worker in metal or rock

My work is with children and women and men –
Not iron, not brass, not wood
And I hope when I lay my stethoscope down
That my Chief will call it good

– Ansel Woodburn

Without question, Grandpa Ansel's Chief called it "good" on March 5, 1968. I shared this poem with Coach, who enjoyed it very much.

I took a sense of inner pleasure thinking – whether rightly or wrongly – that perhaps Ansel's poem had touched Coach enough that he had it in mind a few years later when he spoke at the Nokia Theater in downtown Los Angeles on June 13, 2008, for what proved to be his final large public appearance. "If heaven exists," Wooden, then ninety-seven, was asked at the event's conclusion, "what would you like God to say when you arrive at the Pearly Gates?"

"Well done," Wooden answered, to great applause.
Two years later his Chief surely called it "well done" and
"good."

Δ

Another of the many poems Coach recited to me was
Glennice Harmon's gem, "They Ask Me Why I Teach":

They ask me why I teach
And I reply,
"Where could I find more splendid company?"
There sits a statesman,
Strong, unbiased, wise,
Another later Webster
Silver-tongued.
And there a doctor
Whose quick, steady hand
Can mend a bone or stem the lifeblood's flow.
A builder sits beside him —
Upward rise the arches of that church he builds wherein
That minister will speak the word of God,
And lead a stumbling soul to touch the Christ.

And all about
A lesser gathering
Of farmers, merchants, teachers,
Laborers, men
Who work and vote and build
And plan and pray into a great tomorrow.
And, I say,
"I may not see the church,

> *Or hear the word,*
> *Or eat the food their hands will grow."*
> *And yet – I may.*
> *And later I may say,*
> *"I knew the lad, and he was strong,*
> *Or weak, or kind, or proud*
> *Or bold or gay.*
> *I knew him once,*
> *But then he was a boy."*
> *They ask my why I teach and I reply,*
> *"Where could I find more splendid company?"*

Coach was certainly splendid company. John Muir, reflecting on meeting – and walking with – Ralph Waldo Emerson in the Yosemite Valley, wrote: "Emerson was the most serene, majestic, sequoia-like soul I ever met. His smile was as sweet and calm as morning light on mountains. There was a wonderful charm in his presence; his smile, serene eye, his voice, his manner, were all sensed at once by everybody. A tremendous sincerity was his."

Such is how I felt about Coach after our first walk together.

Before kindly seeing me out to my car after, he gave me a small card featuring his "Pyramid of Success" printed in blue on one side and on the reverse a "Seven-Point Creed" for "Making The Most of One's Self" that his father Joshua had originally written out and given to Johnny when he was 12 years old:

> *Be true to yourself.*
> *Make each day your masterpiece.*
> *Help others.*
> *Drink deeply from good books.*
> *Make friendship a fine art.*
> *Build shelter against a rainy day.*
> *Pray for guidance and give thanks for your blessings every day.*

Ever since, for twenty-six years and counting, I have religiously kept that well-worn card in my wallet. It is my own cherished totem, much like the silver cross that Coach always kept in his pocket.

Three

More Visits

———

"Make friendship a fine art."
– John Wooden

Δ

Next time I joined Coach for a brisk walk, I did something I embarrassingly neglected to do in all my excitement the first time: I brought a gift of thanks for his hospitality. Knowing his love of poetry, I decided a book of poems would be appropriate. My initial thought was to give a collection by Robert Frost, whom I studied in college and enjoyed greatly. Upon further thought, however, I reasoned Coach might already have most, if not all, of Frost's works. So, with the help of an employee at Barnes & Noble, I selected a volume by Rumi. Interestingly, and without any mention by me of this gift, the Persian mystic would years later become my son's favorite poet.

     Coach thanked me for the book while insisting a gift was completely unnecessary. Shortly after I received a handwritten thank-you note; included within was a postcard-sized printed poem authored by Wooden:

On Friendship

At times when I am feeling low,
I hear from a friend and then

My worries start to go away
And I am on the mend

No matter what the doctors say –
And their studies never end

The best cure of all, when spirits fall,
Is a kind word from a friend

Even more prized than the signed poem is that over the ensuing years Coach would turn the words into deed when my spirits fell – particularly when my mom passed away and later when I was severely injured by a speeding drunk driver.

Even when my spirits were already high, Coach had a gift for raising them further. For example, when I next visited him he recited a poem from the Rumi volume I had given him many months previously. I must confess I did not know whom Coach was quoting until he told me. It was not surprising, however, that his selection was titled

"Love" since Coach always insisted it was the most important word in the English language.

Love

Love makes bitter things sweet.
Love turns copper to gold.
With love dregs settle into clarity.
With love suffering ceases.
Love brings the dead back to life.
Love transforms the King into a slave.
Love is the consummation of Gnosis.
How could a fool sit on such a throne?

Visit the sick, and you will heal yourself.
The ill person may be a Sufi master,
And your kindness will be repaid in wisdom.
Even if the sick person is your enemy,
You will still benefit,
For kindness has the power to transform
Sworn enemies into firm friends.
And if there is no healing of bad feeling,
There certainly will be less ill will,
Because kindness is the greatest of all balms.

– Rumi

What a thoughtful and eloquent gesture, what rare grace. It was a simple reminder that saying "thank you" is nice, but to show thanks is even better. Write a note of thanks, certainly, but also wear a new sweater or necklace the next time you see the person who gave it to you; put a gift vase on proud display before the giver comes over; memorize a poem or line from a book given to you. Time and again in ways big and small, Coach put into practice the fifth rule printed on his father's seven-point creed: "Make friendship a fine art."

Through my daily actions and words I have tried to embody his shining example. I donated blood platelets when my beloved sister-like friend Karen Hart Haight was battling an extremely fierce cancer. I make an effort to reach out with a kind word on the phone, with a mailed card, by email, or even with a text message to lift friends' spirits when they are feeling low as well as offer congratulations on their high points. Like any art, the art of friendship must be practiced routinely and without want of something in return. Also, to borrow from the Pyramid of Success, it should not merely be done with a spirit of *willingness* but rather with *eagerness*. Nor must acts of friendship necessarily be grand; as Coach shared, "Woody, sometimes the smallest gestures make the biggest difference."

A small gesture I made a few years ago with no thought of receiving something in return made a big difference in my life by leading to a new, and dear, friendship. After reading a newspaper feature about Ventura author Ken McAlpine and his then-new book, *Islands Apart: A Year on the Edge of Civilization*, I bought it and read it – and loved it. A few weeks later, however, the local newspaper ran an extremely mean-spirited Letter-to-the-Editor that took harsh aim at both the book and McAlpine. In truth, it appeared the nasty critic had not even read *Islands Apart* but rather had a personal axe to grind and wished to uncivilly tear apart its author.

While I did not know McAlpine – surprising, in hindsight, since we live only six miles apart, are both writers, and share numerous interests as well as a handful of friends – I rushed to his defense with my own Letter-to-the-Editor rebuttal that ran a few days later. It was by all measures a small gesture and yet one that I soon learned made a big difference. Indeed, McAlpine's lovely wife, Kathy, later confided that the original letter had wounded her husband but my supportive response in the paper had been a curing balm.

A few weeks before meeting Kathy, I was introduced to Ken by a mutual acquaintance who had seen my letter in print and thought the two of us should meet. Too, the conduit was certain Ken and I would hit it off and thus arranged for us to join him for lunch. To say we hit it off is an understatement; almost overnight Ken became one of my dearest friends. As E.B. White wrote in *Charlotte's Web*: "It is not often that someone comes along who is a true friend and a good writer." In truth, Ken is a *fantastic* writer and I dare say an even better person who – like my longtime brother-like friend Keven Baxter – is a Rembrandt in the art of friendship.

I still find it difficult to believe my great fortune in Coach becoming my friend, my surrogate grandfather almost, my role model and my mentor. The amazing thing is that I was largely the *rule* and not the *exception*; Coach made most everyone who crossed his path feel special. For good reason famed broadcaster Dick Enberg once said: "God has never made a perfect man, but he sure came close with Coach Wooden."

One of Coach's many exceptional qualities was how he made people feel special by giving each individual he was interacting with his undivided attention. For example, he was perhaps the slowest, and surely the most gracious, autograph-signer in history because he made a conscious effort to engage each fan in a brief conversation – and in the process made him or her forget there were others waiting behind in line.

While I never stopped getting slightly nervous as I dialed the phone to call Coach, afterwards I always wondered why I had worried because not once did he fail to greet me warmly. And, to the point made above about giving his full attention, he never seemed in a hurry to hang up. Indeed, if Coach was too busy to talk he would simply not answer the phone in the first place rather than risk the prospect of having to be in a rude rush. For example, I fondly remember visiting Coach when the phone rang and he let the call go through to his answering machine. The message this conveyed was that I was his guest and thus merited his complete focus. This unspoken kindness became even greater seconds later after the "*Beep!*" when a very familiar voice could be heard leaving a message.

"That's Bill Walton!" I said, excitedly. "You'd better answer it!"

Coach did not move towards the phone and instead replied with a devilish smile: "Heavens no! Bill calls me all the time. If I pick up he'll talk my ear off for half an hour and then you and I won't get to visit. I'll talk with him later." And then Coach resumed visiting with me, his attention one-hundred-percent on me.

The great 19th Century American essayist and philosopher Ralph Waldo Emerson once wrote, "A friend may well be reckoned the masterpiece of nature." I love this quote because it epitomizes Coach Wooden's belief in the value of friendship and brings to mind my favorite of all his adages: "Make each day your masterpiece." Certainly each day I visited Coach, talked with him on the phone or received a letter from him, was a masterpiece among masterpiece days.

Four

Fatherhood

―――

"Parenting is the most important profession."
– John Wooden

Δ

I shared happy word with Coach that I had become a father much sooner than anticipated. The exciting news, just two months after our first morning walk, was also terrifying: Dallas Nicole Woodburn was born thirteen weeks prematurely in May rather than August. She weighed a tiny, sickly two pounds, six ounces.

It was a difficult and frightening time to say the least. For a number of weeks Lisa's doctor had been concerned about her high blood pressure and was monitoring it closely. He soon told her she had to rest at home and could no longer go to classes – she was nearing final exams to earn a Masters degree at Cal Poly San Luis Obispo which was about a half-hour drive away. Still her blood pressure rose and other complications joined the party: Lisa, twenty-eight, was in the throes of toxemia, also called preeclampsia. Suddenly one afternoon, in a matter of just a couple hours, her blood pressure spiked and matters turned critical; her body was attacking the fetus within her as though it were a foreign body or infection.

An emergency Cesarean section was needed to save Lisa's life – and, prayerfully, the life of the baby. Santa Maria Valley Community Hospital, without a Neonatal Intensive Care Unit, was ill-equipped to handle the dire situation. A four-person team of specialists was flown in from Fresno's Children's Valley Hospital to perform the delivery and, if all went well and prayers were answered, transport the newborn back with them to Fresno's state-of-the-art NICU facility.

After Lisa was rolled into the Operating Room the wait was interminable. My parents were hours away in Ventura and Lisa's parents were further away in the San Francisco Bay Area; I anxiously paced and sat and paced as my good friend and newspaper colleague Stephen Dana kept me company and tried to lift my spirits, if only marginally. Eventually a nurse came out of the O.R. with an update – not about Lisa or the baby, but merely with the news that the surgical team from Fresno had finally arrived. My heart sped up even more; time slowed even further. The anxious waiting was just beginning.

At long last a doctor came out to say I was the new father of a daughter and that she was "a real fighter." She would need to be; and so would Lisa. Indeed, my wife would remain in the ICU for three days. So perilous was Lisa's condition that two months later when my mother-in-law was visiting her new granddaughter, now safely back in the hospital in Santa Maria, and mentioned to one of the doctors that Dallas' survival had been a miracle, he replied: "Your *daughter* was the miracle."

Lisa had begged for anesthesia because she did not want to be awake and *not* hear a newborn's cry, but because she had eaten within hours of the surprise turn of events this was not possible. Holding her baby also proved impossible because both mother and daughter required immediate emergency care.

While Lisa remained in the Operating Room, the surgical team rolled a high-tech NICU incubator-on-wheels out the O.R. doorway and through the hallway towards the ambulance bay to go to the airport and fly back to Fresno two-hundred-and-fifty miles away. The lifesaving crew stopped its rush, briefly, to allow me to see my daughter. And, in one of the kindest acts I have ever experienced and surely ever will, a nurse opened one of the round portals and told me to place my hand on Dallas' tiny fragile skinny body. In the coming days and weeks I would have to scrub my hands with disinfecting medical soap for a full three minutes before visiting Dallas in the NICU in Fresno, but presently there was no time for that.

The angelic nurse explained, calmly but quickly, that Dallas had not yet felt human skin-to-skin contact because Lisa had been unable, and the medical team of course wore surgical gloves. The nurse added that human touching was vital. Her tone and penetrating eyes delivered an unspoken message too: "This might be the only opportunity your daughter will ever have to feel such contact." And mine to touch Dallas.

The nurse opened the round portal and thermal air rose out as I nervously reached into the Plexiglas womb, carefully avoiding the wires and monitors, and gently placed my hand on Dallas' stomach: her skin was warm and supremely soft and felt wonderful. It remains to this day arguably the most magical and spiritual moment in my entire life.

This will sound melodramatic, but it is also truly what I felt during those too-few seconds: *Dallas is going to make it*. And I specifically did think "Dallas" because while Lisa and I had not yet settled on a boy's name, we had already agreed on Dallas if it were a girl in honor of my father's middle name which is also a family name reaching back at least six generations. Having already selected the name suddenly seemed a paramount blessing to me because there was a very real possibility that Lisa and I otherwise would need to do so posthumously. *Lisa and I?* The truth is I was terrified that my young family of three could at any moment tragically become just one – me. Too soon the precious skin-to-soul visit was up and they whisked Dallas away towards the ambulance that would rush her to the airport where a chartered plane was waiting to transport her to Fresno where these same medical heroes would try to save her life and make my presage – *Dallas is going to make it* – prove true.

I followed in their wake down the hallway and then followed right behind in my car as the ambulance made the short drive to the Santa Maria Airport. As the ambulance made a final turn into a restricted area where I could not go, I vividly remember thinking about Coach Wooden and his bowed head at our breakfast just a couple months earlier. I drew a sense of calm from knowing how strong and true his faith was, and completely out of character I said aloud in a whisper that cracked with emotion, "Godspeed, Dallas, Godspeed" and had an even stronger sense of *knowing* she was going to make it and be healthy without lasting complications.

Lisa was moved out of the ICU after three days and came home from the hospital shortly after that. However, it was touch-and-go for a number of weeks if Dallas would survive, much less thrive. Each morning I would phone the hospital's NICU desk to get the overnight update on how she was doing – in truth, to learn if she had lived through the night. Once the tallest hurdles were cleared, such as potential heart surgery blessedly not being needed and the respirator coming off as her tiny lungs developed, I called Coach and told him the wonderful news. I also sent him my column from June 21, 1987, about her difficult premature birth.

Δ

Rooting My Heart Out For Underdog Dallas

I have a thing for underdogs.

I root for the town against the flood, Tokyo against Godzilla, a canary against a cat. Any team versus the Yankees. Lungs to beat cancer.

I root for Nicklaus and Kareem and Chrissie to beat Father Time. I root for flowers to stay in bloom, snowmen not to melt. Summers not to end.

Give me David, not Goliath. In a movie, I'll root for the ribbon clerk to get the girl. I love the Spud Webbs of the world.

At the top of my list put Dallas.

No, no, no, not the Cowboys. I loathe "America's Team." The special spot in my heart belongs to *Dallas Nicole*.

Dallas came into this world as the longest of long shots. The ultimate underdog. For once, I do not exaggerate. No hyperbole. When you are born three months prematurely the bookmakers do not even list a line. She arrived against all odds.

You see, Dallas's mom was stricken with preeclampsia. A dreaded collection of syllables, preeclampsia is a condition that threatens unborn babies as surely as a blind-side blitz does a quarterback. This time, modern medicine could not pick up all the onrushing linebackers.

With all the receivers covered, Dallas was forced to scramble out of the pocket, so to speak – thirteen weeks before the ball was supposed to even be snapped. Fran Tarkenton never evaded such a heinous pass rush.

So instead of a late August snap count, Dallas was hiked into action on May 29 at 8:34 p.m. I guess she just could not wait to get on with the game of life.

"She's a real fighter," one of the doctors said after Dallas was delivered in an emergency Cesarean section at Santa Maria Valley Community Hospital. A fighter indeed, in the featherweight division at two pounds, six ounces.

A surgical team of specialists were flown in from Fresno to deliver Dallas. Afterwards, the cutting crew took the 15-1/2-inch-long challenger back with them to Children's Valley Hospital where its first-rate Neonatal

Intensive Care Unit could give her a fighting chance to go the distance.

Inside the NICU, banks of electronic gadgetry, plastic tubes, colored wires and around-the-clock care turn Plexiglas breadboxes into counterfeit uteruses for preemies.

A week ago today, two weeks following her birth after her mother finally left the ICU and was discharged from the hospital and could travel, I visited my little MVP – Most Vulnerable Person – for the first time. She is unbelievably tiny. If it were not for the IV and feeding tubes, the EKG wires and the respirator hookup, Dallas could sleep comfortably in a catcher's mitt.

To tell the truth, I hardly noticed all the life-support paraphernalia. I was too busy gazing at the delicate facial features, the bright eyes and wispy auburn hair, the perfectly formed ten fingers and ten toes, each more delicate than a wee tiny flyfishing fly.

But Dallas is not as fragile as she appears. She has been off all medication for over a week now and her IV has been out for nearly as long. Wednesday she KO'd the respirator after three weeks – much sooner than expected. Like the doc said, *She's a real fighter.*

The world may have greeted her with an oh-and-two count, but Dallas has worked it to full. A game-winning homer now seems to be in the cards; the same hand that nearly four long weeks ago looked like a busted eight-high straight.

Yes, the little QB – Qute Baby – converted fourth-and-long yardage into a first down. She didn't have the arm for it, really, but she had the heart, certainly. The storm clouds are clearing. Mommy is fine. From here on out it is going to be rainbows for Dallas. Life will be an endless string of tap-ins for birdie, forty-serving-loves, proms and roses and four-leaf clovers.

The little featherweight is up to two pounds, eleven ounces. That is a monumental gain. When she gets to be a heavyweight of five pounds, Dallas will get to come home. That will be the best belated Father's Day present ever.

Before leaving the NICU last Sunday, I reached into Dallas's womb with a view. Instinctively, I suppose, my favorite little underdog wrapped her teeny hand around the tip of my index finger. For her, it was like palming a basketball. She did not let go for ten minutes, although to this rookie dad it seemed like hours.

Ironic, isn't it? I mean before you know it – if not already – Dallas Nicole Woodburn will have *me* wrapped around *her* finger.

Δ

A few days later a nine-by-twelve-inch manila envelope

arrived in the mail and inside was a Pyramid of Success inscribed to her and predated with her birth date:

> *For Dallas Nicole,*
>
> *With best wishes and the hope that you will grow up into a world of enduring peace between all nations and true love among all people.*
>
>

Love,
John Wooden
May 29, 1987

The thought was as beautiful as the script it was written in. And so perfectly Coach – "peace" and "love." I can imagine no memorabilia was ever more instantly and deeply cherished. Well, not until two and a half years later when, after a far less worrisome birth, a similar Pyramid of Success with a similar inscription arrived as a gift to my newborn son:

> *For Gregory Ansel,*
>
> *With my best wishes and my hope that you will grow up into a world of enduring peace between all nations and true love among all people.*
>
>

Love,
John Wooden
12-22-1989

Included with each Pyramid of Success birthday gift was another keepsake for Dallas and then Greg: a small silver cross. Additionally, after my son's birth Coach sent me a kind letter with "special congratulations to your entire family on the arrival of Gregory Ansel" along with a life lesson he had long cherished in the form of a poem, author unknown, titled: "The Little Fellow Who Follows Me."

"The original of this was presented to me in 1936 upon the birth of my son and has been kept nearby since then," Coach wrote on the enclosed photocopied poem that I, too, have kept nearby – and in mind – ever since:

The Little Fellow Who Follows Me

A careful man I want to be,
A little fellow follows me;
I dare not to go astray,
For fear he'll go the self-same way.

I cannot once escape his eyes,
Whatever he sees me do, he tries;
Like me he says he's going to be,
The little chap who follows me.

He thinks that I am good and fine,
Believes in every word of mine;
The base in me he must not see,
The little chap who follows me.

I must remember as I go,
Through summer's sun and winter's snow;
I am building for the years to be
That little chap who follows me.

Those words have gained growing importance to me with each passing year, not only because Dallas and Greg became more aware of my actions as they grew from toddlers into young children into young adults, but because I became more and more aware that I had become the fellow trying to emulate John Wooden.

Five

My Favorite Teacher

———

"Mentoring is your true legacy. It is the greatest inheritance
you can give to others – to teach and be taught."
– John Wooden

Δ

Like most of us, I suspect, I have been blessed with some
terrific teachers during my lifetime including a very select
few who were true life-changers. The first who comes to
mind was my sixth-grade teacher Mrs. Hutchings at
Windermere Elementary School in Upper Arlington, Ohio.

Mrs. Hutchings challenged me to be a leader with
my voice, not just through my actions. "I would like to see
Woody be less of an independent entity in the classroom
and more inclined to lead his fellow man," she wrote on my
report card in 1972. Part of the problem for me was that for
the first time ever neither of my two best friends, Jim
Hendrix and Dan Means, was in my class. Kindly, however,

she also offered praise: "He has a delightful sense of humor and a sense of fair play that is very unusual for his age."

According to that report card I was the "best student in math" in Mrs. Hutchings' class that year and scored nationally in the 99th percentile – although in college, in Calculus specifically, I think I fell to about the 19th percentile. She further noted my shortcomings in English, which is ironic since by high school this would far exceed math as my strongest subject: "Woody does an outstanding job on reports but his vocabulary words and spelling limit his grades." Indeed, vocabulary was my poorest national test score, in the 68th percentile. Despite this deficiency, Mrs. Hutchings encouraged me to be the editor of the "newspaper" that she helped our class put out that spring. Perhaps this was also her way of encouraging me to be a more vocal leader. Apparently it succeeded to some extent for she noted in June beneath the earlier "independent entity" comment: "I see a definite improvement."

I do not recall what we named our classroom newspaper, but I do clearly remember that Mrs. Hutchings typed the stories into narrow columns. After we used scissors to cut out the individual stories she showed us how to glue them in place on our mock-up page using rubber cement; this made it possible to pull the stories off easily without any tearing in order to move the text around until the "puzzle" fit together the way we wanted.

Following that school year, my dad took Horace Greeley's famous "Go West" advice and moved our family from central Ohio to Southern California – specifically Ventura, which is just sixty miles north of UCLA.

While the move was exciting for my three siblings and me, in hindsight I imagine my parents must have felt much as John and Nell Wooden did when they packed up and left Indiana for Southern California and UCLA. Like Coach, my dad's Midwestern roots went deep. Indeed, Pop's family roots in Ohio reach down, down, down into the fertile farmland and back in time predating the Revolutionary War. But after Grandpa Ansel passed away in 1968, my dad – an only child – felt the roots give way a little under the pull of his dearest friend from medical school, who expounded on the beauty of Ventura and the virtues of its community hospital.

And so "Go West" we did. A full three decades later I received a pleasant surprise in my mailbox; a letter from Mrs. Hutchings, now retired, who had seen my long-form feature story "The Toughest Miler Ever" about American Olympian, World War II hero and POW survivor Louie Zamperini that appeared in the anthology *The Best American Sports Writing 2001*. She praised the piece and said she was proud and thrilled to learn I had become a writer. I wrote back and told her, much too belatedly, that she had been a very special teacher in my life. In fact, I shared the words Coach Wooden had sent to me in response to my first column about him: *Although it is often used without true feeling, when it is used with sincerity, no collection or words can be more expressive or meaningful than the very simple word –* Thanks!

In middle school, I had another life-changing teacher in Harold McFadden. I had "Coach Mac" – as he was called by students and faculty alike – for Physical Education in five of my six semesters at Balboa Junior High.

As often happens, even with our dearest mentors, we fall out of touch and such was the case with Coach Mac. It saddens me to this day that I did not stop by my old school to see him during my visits home to Ventura after I went off to college and beyond.

One day, many years later, I finally returned to the Balboa grounds. And it was like being awakened by the telephone at three o'clock in the morning; like having a police officer knock on your door at dinnertime. You instinctively know it is not good news. It is bad news. Terrible news.

And so it was that my heart raced double-time and pounded in terror as I literally read the writing on the wall: McFADDEN GYM.

Ring . . . ring . . . ring . . .
Knock-knock-knock.
Terrible news.

Gymnasiums and football stadiums are similar to statues and monuments. The latter are chiseled and sculpted and erected to honor fallen heroes; the former are christened or renamed in honor of deceased champions of sport.

I hoped against hope that McFadden Gym was the rare exception to the rule. I prayed for this exception, for positively I knew whom the gym was named after: Harold R. McFadden. Coach Mac. My favorite gym teacher – in fact, one of my favorite teachers, period – of all time.

For the most part, the names of the teachers I had when I roamed Balboa in the early 1970s are lost in cobwebs in a back corner of my mind. Oh, sure, I remember my inspiring shop teacher, Mr. Howell. And the tough-as-cornhusk-but-fair-as-rain Mrs. Stewart, whom I had for various English classes four semesters in a row.

But Coach McFadden was more special. He was a diamond among rhinestones. A star among moons. He was an MVP if the teaching profession gave out such an award. Simply put, when I think of Balboa, I think of Coach Mac.

And when I think of Coach Mac, I instantly think of athletic shoes. Squeaky clean, fresh-out-of-the-shoebox-new sneakers. For the better part of three years I had the great fortune to see Coach Mac every school day. And every day, sunshine or rain, he had on a new pair of athletic shoes.

Or so it seemed.

Actually, he only broke out a fresh pair of footwear three or four times a year. Christmas presents and birthday presents, he once told me. But he had more than a dozen old pairs of athletic shoes that *looked* brand spankin' new. Maybe twenty pairs. His secret, he shared gladly, was to clean them after every wearing – just like my Grandpa Ansel used to do with his wingtip dress shoes. But instead of shoe polish and a soft cloth and a shining brush, Coach Mac found that a soft worn-out toothbrush and a squirt of liquid dishwashing soap, plus a dab of elbow grease, did the trick nicely.

So it just appeared as though Coach Mac wore *new* shoes every day: red suede Converse All-Stars low-tops on Monday; red-white-and-blue Tigers (now called Asics) running shoes on Tuesday; UCLA Bruin blue Chuck Taylor Converse high-tops on Wednesday; Adidas Superstars with red stripes on Thursday and Supertsars with blue stripes on Friday; white-and-blue Nikes Cortez the next Monday . . .

There was much more to Coach Mac than his immaculate size-ten shoes. He cast an imposing figure as a P.E. teacher and role model. Even back then, four decades ago, he was coaching kids to say no to drugs. Imploring us to hit the books, not just the basketball backboards and pitches in the strike zone. Most of all, he encouraged us to *try*. Like Coach Wooden, Coach Mac wanted his charges to be the best we were capable of being.

The stereotypical gym coach is a droll drillmaster. Simon Legree with a clipboard and whistle. Coach McFadden was cut from a different sweatshirt cloth. He never raised his voice, never frowned, never was at a loss for warm words. He whipped his students into shape with kindness, with encouragement, with guile. He made the medicine taste like a spoonful of sugar.

I vividly recall that he used to add one more push-up every week during our warm-up calisthenics and by the end of the semester even the out-of-shape couch potatoes could get down and do twenty.

Coach Mac swayed selfish gunners to play selfless team-style basketball. Some kids he turned on to wrestling, others on to track or soccer. Every kid he tried to inspire into something athletic. If you could not be a "Bullet Bob" Hayes-like sprinter then be a Distance Demon, he encouraged. If you cannot sprint all the way to the far fence of the schoolyard and back, run there and walk back. *Try.* Be the best you can be. That makes you a true success.

One yardstick for any junior high gym instructor is the number of students who do not dress out for class. Coach Mac's classes, I am convinced, set the standard for the lowest number of non-dressers in P.E. history. Why would anyone want to fake a medical excuse to get out of having fun?

I must admit that Coach Mac was not perfect. He

never did get me to do a respectable handstand, for instance. But my sneakers always looked newer thanks to him. They still do. Indeed, for the last forty years, every time I have meticulously laced up a brand-new pair of athletic shoes I have thought of Coach Mac. Also while scrubbing a dirty pair of running shoes with an old toothbrush and dishwashing soap and, of course, some elbow grease – the same recipe my son now uses to clean thousands of athletic shoes before donating them to impoverished youth around the globe through his charity foundation "Give Running." Even seeing new sneakers on someone else, or walking by a Footlocker store, brings Coach Mac to my mind.

Ring . . . ring . . . ring . . .

Knock-knock-knock.

My worst fear proved well-founded. After seeing his name on the gym and doing some research, I found out that Coach McFadden died in 1984, exactly ten years after my final P.E. class with him and long before he had a chance to lose the hop on his fastball, the shrill in his whistle. He was far too young at age fifty-four. Finding out a decade after his passing did not lesson the heartbreak and loss.

I am glad my old junior high re-christened its gym after Harold R. McFadden. It is even more heartening to know that it became "Mac's Gym," as it is most often called, a year *before* Coach McFadden succumbed, after a gallant battle, to two of the most heinous syllables in the English language: *can-cer*. Indeed, it is pleasing to know that Coach Mac lived to see McFADDEN GYM christened in his honor, for as Felicia Hyams once wrote: "Roses to the living are better than sumptuous wreaths to the dead."

As mentioned, at Balboa Junior High School I also had the great fortune to have Mrs. Stewart for two full years of English classes. Looking back, I think it was in her classroom that the seed to become a writer was perhaps planted. That seed was watered my freshman year at the University of California at Santa Barbara by John Ridland, an English professor I had for "The Poetry of Robert Frost."

Professor Ridland loved not just good poetry but all good writing, and he helped give me a new appreciation for the sound of the written word: the beauty of cadence and rhythm, the power of repetition, the importance of word choice and so much more. While I sometimes felt lost in an iambic labyrinth trying to understand Mr. Frost, Mr. Ridland's positive comments on my essays throughout the semester gave me growing confidence as a writer.

After I suffered an athletic injury that proved stubborn in healing, and thus eventually had to quit the UCSB tennis team, I saw a small "Help Wanted" ad in *The Daily Nexus* student newspaper seeking a sportswriter. I asked Professor Ridland what he thought of the idea and he enthusiastically encouraged me to apply – and, I later learned, also put in a good word on my behalf to the sports editor without my request. I got the job and, considering my grandfather, father and two older brothers all became physicians, I think it is fitting to quote the final stanza in Frost's "The Road Not Taken" to describe my life journey as a result:

> *I shall be telling this with a sigh*
> *Somewhere ages and ages hence:*
> *Two roads diverged in a wood, and I –*
> *I took the one less traveled by,*
> *And that has made all the difference.*

My Favorite Teacher Ever, however, the one who truly made all the difference, was in my post-graduate studies "Life 101" class taught by Professor John Robert Wooden. Our classroom was not a lecture hall nor basketball court, but instead was Coach's home on some occasions and walks around his neighborhood on others. Phone calls and personal letters extended the curriculum into part correspondence course; his numerous published works served as textbooks.

In addition, I attended a handful of public lectures given by Professor Wooden, including taking my dear friend-surrogate-cousin Jimmy Hart to an enchanting evening at the historic Pasadena Civic Center where Coach captivated a full house with his witty stories, uncommon enlightenment and numerous poems, all offered as a friendly conversation without notes. Just twelve miles away by freeway but more than a decade later at Wooden's final marquee lecture at the sold-out Nokia Theatre in Los Angeles in December 2008, three generations of Woodburn men savored a night for the ages. Coach's body was by now failing and he needed a wheelchair, but his mind remained as keen and quick as ever.

To be sure, one did not have to play for Coach Wooden in order to be one of his students and of this I am a privileged example. I was not one of his basketball players – except for one glorious week at youth camp – but make no mistake, I was his pupil. No coach or teacher or professor has taught me more, or taught me more-important things.

Six

The Little Ones

———

"Love is nothing unless we give it to someone."
– John Wooden

Δ

Looking back, I believe there were a number of reasons, beyond his uncommonly deep well of kindness, why Coach found room, and time, in his life for me. For one, I met him just as he was climbing out from the deepest depths of his mourning over Nellie's death and rejoining the outside world.

Also, I came knocking, so to speak, before he reemerged in the national spotlight as a best-selling author, highly sought-after lecturer, basketball professor emeritus, Dalai Lama-like guru, humanitarian and downright national treasure – in 2003 Wooden would receive the United States Presidential Medal of Freedom, the highest honor given to a civilian in recognition of especially meritorious contributions.

And so, quite simply, when I first interviewed Coach in San Luis Obispo and then gradually sought his mentorship and friendship through letters, phone calls, morning walks and visits, he had the time; his phone was not yet ringing off the hook with reporters and his mailbox was not yet overflowing daily with autograph requests. As years passed, his answering machine began to work overtime during my visits and the mailman would leave – and pick up – a laundry basket-sized plastic bin, often filled above the brim.

Above all, however, I think the two biggest reasons we connected as we did were my two "Little Ones" who were born around the same time Wooden's great-grandchildren began arriving. Pulling further on his heartstrings were Dallas and Greg's older sister/younger brother birth order which, Coach pointed out with pleasure, was the same as with his two children, Nan and James. Perhaps to a small degree Coach saw some of his family in mine. Too, I believe Coach later felt a special bond with Dallas because of the trying conditions of her birth and the fact that his first great-grandchild, about one year older than my daughter, had her own medical challenges after being diagnosed with juvenile diabetes around age five.

And so – whether for a column about the NCAA Tournament draw or UCLA's basketball program or the

NBA; or, as became the case more frequently over time, simply to say hello and "visit" by phone – whenever I called Coach his first response without fail upon hearing my voice would be: "How are the Little Ones?" I would give him updates on Dallas and Greg, and then in turn ask about his Little Ones and he would tell me about his great-grandchildren. Before hanging up he often reminded me about one of his core beliefs for parenting: "Being a role model is the most powerful way of teaching."

Part of being a good parental role model, Coach said, is to make your children a priority and give them your time. "Even little acts of fun and patience can be extremely meaningful," he emphasized after I sent him the column below that I wrote about flying a kite with Dallas when she was still a very Little One.

Δ

A Tale of a Kite Without A Tail

"The wind is fast," the little girl announced excitedly, half out of breath from racing inside and upstairs. "Can we fly my kite?"

The little girl had gotten her very first kite a few weeks before and had patiently waited for an afternoon that wasn't too calm or too rainy or too windy. This day, she hoped, like Little Bear's porridge, was "just right."

The father looked at the treetops dancing in the breeze. "Go get your kite," he said, smiling.

They walked to the park, hand-in-hand, the blonde little girl pretty in pink and as excited as if she were coming down the stairs on Christmas morning.

The little girl's kite cost all of 99 cents (with a spool of cotton string included in the bargain) but it had something the more-expensive models did not have – a rainbow on its plastic skin. The little girl, you should know, dearly loves rainbows.

Kites of paper, like those the father used to fly when he was the little girl's age – "three, almost four" – are impossible to find nowadays, as are kites shaped like kites ought to be shaped, that is, like a diamond, taller than wide. The little girl's kite was wider than tall, like an eagle with wings spread.

"Let's go fly a kite . . ." sang the little girl, now skipping and now wearing her father's too-large-for-her "Johnny Bench hat," as she calls his Cincinnati Reds baseball cap. ". . . and send it soaring. Up to the highest height. Up through the atmosphere . . ."

When the kite was soaring up where the air is clear, the father let the little girl take hold of the string.

"Wow! Neat! Cool!"

The little girl was also excited.

"It feels like catching a big fish in the sky," she said, a wonderful observation considering the little girl has never felt the tug of a fish. (Her father, by the way, too often doesn't feel a fish's tug either.)

Then the kite took a nosedive and crashed to earth like a kamikaze going down a ship's smokestack.

Fortunately, it escaped damage.

The little girl sprinted to the fallen kite as if an Olympic gold medal were at stake, picked it up and counted "One-two-three!" before letting go as the father pulled on the string. The kite again quickly soared up to the highest height.

Then another kamikaze crash. And another Olympic sprint. "One-two-three!" Once more the rainbow kite soared up where the air is clear before once more crashing.

"Your kite needs a tail," the father remarked.

"A tail?" the little girl echoed quizzically, rolling her eyes and giggling. "Daddy, you bingo-bum (her own made-up word for a silly person). Kites don't have tails – doggies and kitty cats and monkeys have tails."

The father laughed and tried to explain that in the "old days" you tied strips of cloth together to make a tail that kept the kite upright and prevented it from crashing. He also warned that you must always be sure to use old rags, that when he was a little boy he once got in trouble for cutting up one of his dad's – uh, Gramps' – good shirts to use as a tail.

This, of course, made the little girl laugh, the idea of her daddy being scolded by Gramps.

With no rags handy, the tail-less rainbow kite was again soaring as high as a rainbow.

SNAP!

The cheap cotton string broke and the kite fluttered away over a row of tall trees.

"Oh no!" the little girl cried out. "It's going into The Gully!"

They hurried hand-in-hand, the father and little girl, to the edge of The Gully and spotted the kite far below – high up in a tree.

The father helped the little girl climb through a gate with a NO TRESPASSING sign posted on it. At the risk of a $500 fine, he was going to get back her 99-cent rainbow.

The father climbed a tree – when was the last time he had done that? Ten years ago? Fifteen maybe? – and rescued the little girl's very first kite, and a small piece of his own childhood in the process.

"Thank you, Daddy," the little girl said happily and sweetly, giving a tight hug and a kiss as reward. Then, examining at the broken string, she added: "I think we need a stronger rope."

The very next day the two went to a kite store to get a stronger "rope."

"That's a pretty one," the little girl said gleefully, surveying a blue-and-red state-of-the-art nylon kite that was nearly as big as a hang glider. "But I like mine better."

The father looked at the price tag: $120! There were also kites for $90 and $49 and $21. But there were no 99-cent kites. No paper kites that need rag tails. No kites shaped like kites ought to be shaped, like diamonds, taller than wide. And, fortunately, no kites the little girl liked better than her own.

She found the "rope" she wanted, the little girl did, 500 feet of nylon string on a plastic yellow spool. Five dollars of "rope" for a 99-cent kite, but the father did not mind in the least.

At the cashier's counter she changed her mind, for that's a little woman's prerogative too.

"I think I want the blue one," she said and skipped off to get the "rope" on a blue spool.

As they were walking hand-in-hand out of the store, the little girl studied all the many kites and then stopped abruptly and looked up at her father.

"Daddy, you bingo-bum!" she giggled. "I told you kites don't have tails. Only animals do."

Δ

Dallas still fondly remembers that afternoon and to this day sometimes playfully calls me "Bingo-bum." Heeding the importance of these fleeting opportunities to share time together when children are young, I made a point to not only do fun things with Dallas and Greg together – like fly kites and play on the swings; go to the library or a movie; ride paddle boats and the merry-go-round at the harbor – but also regularly spend one-on-one time with each child. For example, I began taking Dallas on dinner "dates" when she was about four years old. We made a big deal of it, too; she would wear a dress and I would put on a sports coat – my "tuxedo" she called it – and always I would give her a rose or a sunflower and open the car door for her.

Similarly, Greg and I enjoyed our own special outings – "Big Grog/Little Grog Time" he called our adventures using our nicknames for each other – that included taking him along with me when I interviewed famous athletes, especially Olympic runners (track being his favorite sport since he was six).

The ideal time for these one-on-one father-child outings with Greg or Dallas was when the other sibling was spending the night with a friend – this way no one ever felt left out. Lisa selflessly encouraged this dad-only time with the kids.

Did these little things make a big difference as Coach suggested? My answer is this: whenever they are both back home Dallas and Greg make a point of having a "breakfast date" with each other on the morning one of them has to leave again. What could make a parent happier than such sibling revelry instead of rivalry?

As Coach and I grew closer, several times I phoned him for advice on personal matters in my own life. One such occasion was when I was offered a position as a sports columnist in Torrance where I would get to cover more big-time events in Los Angeles than I was currently getting the opportunity to do. The downside would be much more time spent away from home as I would have a lengthy commute to sporting events in L.A. or the newspaper's offices in Torrance. As was my ultimate consideration in turning down an earlier job offer in Philadelphia, I did not want to move Dallas and Greg away from their close friends and familiar schools and tight family ties with their cousins and Gramps, nor ask Lisa to leave a job she enjoyed and found fulfilling. So relocating to Torrance was not an option on the table.

I should have anticipated Coach's response, for it was something he preached often. He reminded me what he considered the two most important words in the English language: *love* and *balance*. Would the new position knock my life – specifically, my family life – out of balance? he asked.

Upon consideration, I realized the extra drive time would largely be added during the early afternoon and late at night – times when I did not usually see Lisa and Dallas and Greg anyway because they were at work and school, or else sleeping. Moreover, I would actually often have either Saturday or Sunday entirely off at the new job whereas I was almost always working both weekend days from late afternoon until midnight helping out with copyediting on the desk at my current paper in Ventura.

Probably the biggest downside, the loss of balance, would be that I would no longer be able to drive home in ten minutes to share a rushed dinner with my family as I currently did most evenings. And yet with Dallas, then thirteen years old and Greg having turned eleven, they were likely to begin missing more and more family dinners themselves with growing schedules of school activities, basketball games and track meets. Perhaps upgrading my cell phone plan with unlimited minutes and talking to the kids every evening would be an effective and happy compromise?

Wooden's true wisdom, however, was this golden nugget of advice: Explain the situation to Dallas and Greg, and ask what they think. By letting them have input in the decision, when those evenings came and they missed me more than usual at dinner they would be less inclined to feel confused or hurt or angry because the situation had not been forced upon them. If they were truly mature enough for the changes brought about by the new job to not adversely affect them, then they would also be mature enough to tell me to accept it.

And that is exactly what happened. I took Dallas and Greg to one of our favorite lunch spots, Duke's Burgers right at the beach, and after we discussed the matter from all angles they told me to go for it – Lisa had already cast the same vote – and never seemed to have any reservations afterwards. Indeed, when those times arose and I could not be home for this game or that meet or some other occasion, they still did not resent my absence because they had helped make the decision and wanted what was best for me.

What a valuable lesson and experience it proved to be for all four of us, because in the end isn't that a key part of what *love* is all about, putting others before yourself?

Seven

Love and Letters

––––

*"The best thing a father can do for his children
is to love their mother."*
– John Wooden,
quoting Abraham Lincoln

Δ

When I think of John Wooden, I think of a man of letters.
The letters U-C-L-A, of course, where he authored such a
remarkable story that included chapters of an eighty-eight
consecutive-game winning streak and ten NCAA titles
overall. But also as a classic "man of letters" – a former
English teacher who always saw himself as an educator
first and foremost.

I also think of the letters Coach wrote on the
twenty-first of each and every month for the final twenty-
five years of his life. He wrote the letters to his wife Nellie,
who died on March 21 – the first day of spring, extra cruelly
– 1985. March Sadness for the man who had once ruled

March Madness by winning those ten NCAA championships in a twelve-year span.

The growing stack of letters rested on their shared bed near her pillow; when Coach passed away the letters numbered more than three-hundred – a streak that is far more amazing than eighty-eight straight basketball victories or seven NCAA championships in a row. Also on the bed Coach kept Nell's robe along with a couple favored photos of her.

"Good things take time," Coach reminded me more than once, "usually a lot of time. And good things should take time." It was a sentiment that truly described his storybook marriage.

Coach and Nell went to thirty-six Final Fours in a row together until she fell ill in December 1984. He took her to the hospital on Christmas morning of all days and she never left. For a number of years after she died he stopped attending the Final Four. So cavernous was Coach's grief that he told me for a long while he was eagerly awaiting life's final buzzer. Blessedly his zest for living came back with the birth of his great-grandchildren, thirteen Little Ones in all at the time of his passing.

"They are really a reason for living," Coach told me, his eyes radiating happiness.

He again expressed to me this growing joy that trumped his indelible sorrow in a letter dated October 25,

1992 – two weeks on the heels of his eighty-second birthday: *". . . I thoroughly enjoyed hearing about and seeing snapshots of the little ones. They change rapidly, but each change is interesting.*

"I now have six great-grandchildren with a seventh on the way and they have become my reason for living since losing my dear Nellie. It helps that they are all near enough that I get to see them at least once each week."

Days later, Coach wrote another letter – this one addressed to my father. Again, Nellie was at the heart of the handwriting.

My mom, only sixty, had died of a sudden heart attack on October 15. My dad never dated anyone else after he met my mom at a barn dance on Friday, October 13 – "a lucky Friday the thirteenth," Pop likes to say – in 1950. They were married for thirty-eight years before she passed. To this day, much like Coach with Nell's bathrobe, my dad keeps one of his sweetheart's sweaters on his bed under her pillow. My parents' wedding anniversary was August 7 – the day before Coach and Nell's.

As I wrote in my eulogy of a column two days later: "When you talk about love affairs, you can begin with this one: Audrey Rahn and James Woodburn. Step aside Romeo and Juliet. It started with a blind date, if you can believe it, and lasted forty-two years – and two days. College sweethearts forever. The petals are still fresh on the first-date anniversary red rose Dad just gave her."

And: "Mom was the Typhoid Mary of Happiness. She was the pinnacle of kindness. The Golden Rule brought to life. She had these big blue eyes, movie-star blue, that were happy and joyful and warm all the time. She never went a full minute without smiling. She lit up every room she entered. Everyone became a nicer person when she was around. And happier. It was contagious."

This, I would learn, was very much how Coach described Nell.

"I'm lucky in that there were no 'I love yous' left unsaid," I wrote at column's end. "Actually, that's not true. There were about a million more to say."

After my mom's death I watched my dad seem to age another full year with each passing day, suffering in the same manner Coach had described his own physical slide and emotional freefall after Nell died. I phoned Coach and asked if he might have a few words of insight and experience that could possibly give my dad some solace and lift his depression, if only slightly.

Dear Dr. Woodburn –

Your son, Woody, just informed me of the passing of your beloved wife and, since I experienced the same situation on March 21,

1985, thought I might be able to add a word of comfort.

Nellie and I were sweethearts for almost sixty years, married for almost fifty-three and I shall never get over her death.

However, after a year or two of mere existence, my pastor, my doctor, my friends, my children, my grandchildren and six great-grandchildren have helped me carry on. I now live for her through the lives of our loved ones and no longer have any fear of death as that is my only chance, if He will forgive me of my sins, to be with her again. I eagerly await that event.

The enclosures are among the many things received from friends that have helped to some degree.

May His love and that of those near and dear to you bring solace and hope in this time of need.

Sincerely,
John Wooden

It was, I believe, the most meaningful condolence card my father received. Coach's heartfelt words were a soothing salve. Pop definitely found a new purpose and happiness through his grandchildren, eight at the time and presently nine. Furthermore, my dad – now eighty-six and still scrubbing in to assist with surgeries two or three days a week – carries the letter, and the enclosures of poem and prayers Wooden included, in his briefcase a full twenty years later.

"I talk to her every day," Coach told me on my first visit, two years to the month after Nell's death, as he gave me a tour of his – their – modest condominium. He casually noted the neat stack of letters tied in a ribbon on the bed and said it was just another way of having a conversation with her, as was talking aloud at her gravesite.

I can only imagine Coach's ever-present displays of deep love and dedication to Nell when she was still alive. Inspired by Coach, and keeping in mind his beliefs that "the best thing a father can do for his children is to love their mother" and "the most effective way to teach is through example," I set out to be a worthy role model for my two children in this area.

When Dallas and Greg were in preschool, I began taking them with me once a month to a local flower stand to buy a single rose – usually yellow because that was the color rose I gave Lisa our first date on December 13, 1980 (my own "lucky thirteen") although sometimes Dallas or Greg would pick out a red or peach or white one. Then we would go to Lisa's office and personally deliver it at her cubicle. If she was in a meeting or out on a site visit, we would leave a loving note along with the rose.

My wife's co-workers quickly went from teasing her about "What did Woody do that he needs to apologize for it with flowers?" to being slightly envious. Lisa, obviously, loved the caring gesture. But the real winners were Dallas and Greg, who saw in this small-and-routine kindness that their father loved their mother. It pleases me, and greatly, that Dallas and Greg fondly and clearly remember our rose ritual and say it has affected how they treat their dates and expect to be treated – not necessarily always with flowers, but with opened car doors and compliments and respect.

I never told Coach about the rose ritual, and probably I should have. However, I did tell him how Lisa and I began our married life together with not a whole lot more than $909.05 to our names. And, like Nell's unconditional support for Coach, when I got my first job after graduating college at a newspaper in the one-stoplight town of Twentynine Palms in the California high desert – I actually got a phone call during our honeymoon and we made a detour driving home for the interview – Lisa never saw it as a year-long hardship. She has always said the isolation was a gift because it brought us even closer together as a couple.

Coach listened as I shared this, smiled, and reminded me of the Friendship block in the Pyramid of Success: "Comes from mutual esteem, respect and devotion. Like marriage it must not be taken for granted but requires joint effort."

Like my Dad and Coach, I have been blessed in love and marriage. I met Lisa at a college Christmas party my sophomore year; she was a junior. I still remember that she was wearing a light blue turtleneck sweater. I strategically maneuvered myself under some mistletoe as we talked, but my ploy failed as she edged away before I could act. We laugh about this inept "move" to this day. But I did kiss her later that night, on her mistletoe-less doorstep.

We dated for barely a year and a half – and that is without subtracting a three-month breakup in the middle of our romance plus a summer spent apart – before I proposed a couple months prior to my graduation. I was 22 and Lisa, who graduated the previous year, was 23.

Oh, yes, and I had not yet even met Lisa's mother when I popped the question. You can just imagine how well the bride-to-be's long-distance phone call home with news of the engagement went over. Understandably her parents, living three thousand miles away, tried to talk her into pushing the wedding date back a year from the upcoming October to the following September. Lisa compromised: she agreed on September – but the upcoming one five months hence. On September 4, 1982 we were wed.

The secret to a successful marriage? Here, on men's behalf, is the best I can come up with: Find a former homecoming princess whose beauty runs deep, deep, deep to a kind soul and caring heart; who is loving and confident and intelligent, charming and generous and strong; who has a sense of humor and an aura of grace; and, importantly, is foolish enough to happily marry someone not within a ZIP Code of being worthy of her hand.

Thirty-two years now – and two children raised to adulthood – is a long time, yet it also seems to have passed in about thirty-two days. The French writer Andre Maurois noted, "A happy marriage is a long conversation that always seems too short." Lisa makes me feel this way.

She also brings to my mind, and heart, this passage from A.A. Milne's *Winnie-the-Pooh* for it describes how I have felt about her almost since the night we met:

"We'll be Friends Forever, won't we, Pooh?" asked Piglet.

"Even longer," Pooh answered.

Δ

The stack of un-mailed love letters grew a little higher each time I visited Coach; each time he also grew a little slower of foot. Arthritis gradually applied a full-court press to his knees and hips. Nicknamed the "Indiana Rubber Man" during his star playing days at Purdue because he would bounce right back up off the floor after diving for a loose ball or getting knocked down, he now had to shorten, and later eventually stop altogether, his beloved morning walks. He needed cortisone shots and physical therapy and ultimately two hip replacements.

"My walking is out, I'm afraid," Coach wrote to me in March 1991 when I asked about joining him once more. "But I've got so I can get along with a cane." That was an improvement from relying on a walker, which he had been forced to do for a while. Yet he still politely insisted on coming to greet me at the front gate when I visited as well as escorting me back out afterward.

Seeing Coach need the aid of a cane made it difficult to imagine he had once been the indestructible Indiana Rubber Man. Indeed, it is often overlooked that before he was a great, great coach, John Wooden was a great, great player. At five-foot-ten and 183-pounds, "Johnny" was a three-time consensus All-American guard at Purdue and named the college Player of the Year in 1932 – the same year my mom was born just one-hundred-and-thirty miles north of the West Lafayette university campus in Oak Park, Illinois.

Coach told me, however, that he was more proud of being the 1932 recipient of the Big Ten Medal for Proficiency in Scholarship and Athletics than he was of being named the nation's Player of the Year.

Wooden went on to be an outstanding professional player for six years during the barnstorming pre-NBA days, once making one-hundred-and-thirty-eight consecutive free throws for the Indianapolis Kautskys spanning the 1934 to 1936 seasons – a mark that still stands as the world record for professional basketball leagues. The NBA record, by comparison, is ninety-seven in a row.

Yes, Wooden really had a penchant for streaks: one-hundred-and-thirty-eight free throws in a row; seven consecutive NCAA titles; eighty-eight straight games won; and most importantly, married to his high school sweetheart for fifty-three years.

Like my dad, whose thoughts never seem to stray for very long from my mom all these years later, Nell always remained front-and-center in Coach's mind and heart. In 2003, Wooden agreed to have UCLA's Pauley Pavilion basketball floor named in his honor – but only if Nell's name was included, and received top billing, because he said he could not have accomplished the feats without her by his side every step of the journey.

On December 20 of that year a special ceremony was held at Pauley Pavilion with 12,433 people in attendance, including seven of Wooden's great-grandchildren and about seventy former players. I, too, would not have missed the occasion for the world. During the festivities on *Nell & John WOODEN COURT*, Coach did what he always made his players do on any basketball floor after they scored – point a finger of acknowledgement at the teammate who helped make the score possible.

"I know what made this day possible," Wooden said as he turned and looked at his former players seated behind the far basket, "these young men down there."

Young men. No matter that many had become senior citizens, to Wooden they would be forever young. Bill Walton, his once flaming-red hair now showing gray, said to me later that day of Coach: "His dignity and stature as a human being are unmatched. He's the greatest teacher ever. He's the master. I love him."

"I love the man," Kareem privately echoed moments later.

This is the one thing I have in common with these two seven-foot-tall Hall-of-Fame legends.

Eight

The Car Crash

"Most worthwhile things come wrapped in adversity."
– John Wooden

Δ

Long before Lance Armstrong was stripped of his seven consecutive Tour de France cycling titles in 2012 for having used performance-enhancing drugs during his record victory streak from 1999-2005, Armstrong's world was famously turned upside down on October 2, 1996. That was the day Armstrong was diagnosed with testicular cancer that had spread to his brain and lungs.

After triumphing over odds stacked heavily against survival, Armstrong has annually celebrated 10/2 as the moment his life changed unexpectedly for the better because he feels his dance with death gave him a new and true appreciation for the music of being alive.

I have my own 10/2, as I believe many of us do in our own lives or through a loved one. Mine happens to be on 1/26. January 26, 2003 was the date of Super Bowl XXXVII in San Diego, which I covered as a newspaper sports columnist. Late that night, a few hours after the Tampa Bay Buccaneers turned the Oakland Raiders into twisted total wreckage, 48-21, an uninsured drunk driver did the same to my silver Honda Accord.

I was stopped at an intersection waiting for two traffic officers to give me the go-ahead to make a right turn. I did not see or hear the car rocketing towards me from behind, but fortunately the two officers standing directly in front of my car did. They moved out of the way just before my Honda was rammed from behind at an estimated sixty-five miles per hour and sent spinning forward through the intersection.

The impact was so violent that my driver's seat was ripped loose, the heavy steel bolts sheared cleanly off. When Lisa phoned the impound company the following morning, she was offered condolences; the employee had seen the metal carnage and assumed I had surely been killed.

"You're a very lucky man," one of the police officers told me the night of the crash after he finished documenting the scene. According to the U.S. National Highway Traffic Safety Administration, 17,013 people were killed in alcohol-related accidents that year (2003). I was beyond lucky that final figure was not 17,014.

Still, luck is relative. I suffered a ruptured disc in my neck and underwent a two-hour operation called an "anterior cervical discectomy and fusion five-six with iliac graft." Translation: a neurosurgeon sliced my neck open from the front, delicately removed the damaged disc between my fifth and sixth vertebrae without injuring the spinal cord, used a power jigsaw to cut a small wedge from my pelvis and then shoehorned this slice of bone between the two vertebrae to allow them to fuse together.

The surgery left a three-inch scar running across my Adam's apple that allows me to honestly tell people who ask about it, "Oh, it's from an old Super Bowl injury." The injury caused nerve damage that has proved irreversible. A full decade later I have chronic neck and shoulder pain while my left thumb and fingers have diminished sensitivity and dexterity. Upon returning to work I found that hunching over a keyboard in a cramped press box became physically tormenting enough to interfere with my concentration after about an hour.

All the same, I annually celebrate my 1/26 anniversary as a blessing.

I came to the slow realization afterward that once again Coach Wooden was so very right: "Things turn out best for those who make the best of the way things turn out." With this mindset, here is how things turned out for the better. To begin, the accident and injuries forced me to leave a job I loved too much to leave on my own. Sportswriting took me away from home most weekend days, too many weeknights, and the majority of holidays.

Yes, I still miss the press box, but in return I have *not* missed so much more. Lisa and I have celebrated our past ten wedding anniversaries *on the correct date*, not on the nearest night on the calendar without a game I had to cover. Instead of being at Dodger Stadium or Staples Center or the Los Angeles Memorial Coliseum, I attended every performance of two plays Dallas wrote and co-directed in high school and two more in college. I did not miss a single one of Greg's high school cross-country or track meets; I missed only one of his meets during his four years competing in both sports at the University of Southern California; and I also made it to three USC art shows exhibiting his paintings. I would not trade covering any number of Super Bowls, NBA Finals and Olympics for half of all those plays and races and shows.

Before the car crash – and I purposefully say *crash* and not *accident* because someone driving drunk is not accidental but rather an irresponsible, dangerous and too-often deadly choice – I did not fully appreciate Coach's advice to "make the best of the way things turn out" and that "most worthwhile things come wrapped in adversity." Even "Make each day your masterpiece," which I feel is a more eloquent version of Johnathan Swift's "May you live every day of your life," took on a more profound meaning after having my life spun around violently by a drunk driver. Ironically, after being knocked off its axis my life gained a better balance.

Sure, there are times when my neck aches more than usual and my afflicted fingers feel ablaze and I feel a momentary twinge of self-pity, silently cursing the drunk driver who escaped any semblance of justice by fleeing the state before appearing in court. Still, by and by the traffic cop was right – I am a very lucky man. I had to give up playing tennis and basketball, but I completed a marathon (in three hours, eighteen minutes) two years after the crash – and I did not have to do so in the wheelchair division. I have since completed a handful more, including the prestigious Boston Marathon in 2009.

It should be no surprise that I gained inspiration from Coach's words, including, "If we magnified blessings as much as we magnify disappointments, we would all be much happier."

Even more so I draw strength from some of his own trials and tribulations, such as losing his life savings to a bank failure the day before his wedding; a heart attack in 1972 from which he returned to coaching; and perhaps most admirable of all, the way he resolutely climbed out of the Grand Canyon-like depths of grief following Nell's death on March 21, 1985 and continued spreading his love and wisdom to family, friends and the world for an additional quarter-century before his own passing.

As much as I lost because of a drunk driver – a portion of my health, my dream job, a good deal of income – at least my life was not lost. In fact, to paraphrase Coach, I was forced to not let making a living prevent me from making a life. Indeed, for everything that was taken away by the crash, I gained even more. Lance Armstrong's 10/2 and Coach's 3/21 and my 1/26 and so many people's personal equivalent of 9/11 should make each of us realize our days are numbered. So try to make each one a masterpiece.

Δ

My days became numbered in a different way following my car crash with the drunk driver. When I returned home from the hospital following my disc fusion surgery, even walking a few steps was agony. It wasn't my neck that caused me to wince; it was the spot on my right pelvis where bone graft was removed to surgically wedge between my fifth and sixth vertebrae.

Before the crash I had completed a large handful of marathons, including the Los Angeles Marathon twice. I was training to run L.A. for a third time that upcoming March 2003, but of course that proved impossible. Running

26.2 miles was now literally a laughable notion. A month after surgery I remember making the short walk to our mailbox with Dallas escorting me, lest I need someone to lean on. As we slowly made our way back up the driveway, which I should point out is sloped more gently than some putting greens, I said to her in total seriousness as my right hip throbbed in pain: "Geez, this is pretty steep."

Simultaneously we broke into laughter at the absurdity of it. Only a few months previously I had run a marathon in three hours, twenty-nine minutes on a challenging course made even more difficult by unseasonable heat in the eighties, and now a mildly inclined driveway felt like Heartbreak Hill at mile twenty-one of the famed Boston Marathon course. I had long dreamed of running the Boston Marathon, but clocking a qualifying time necessary to earn entry was now about the furthest thing from my mind. At this moment, with a limp in my step and a soft collar brace around my neck, I could not even imagine jogging around the block.

Again, Coach's homespun wisdom buoyed my spirits and provided perspective: "Don't let what you cannot do interfere with what you can do." If I could not run, I could walk – a little more distance, and a little less timidly, each day. It was the same tactic and emphasis on trying that Coach Mac had employed with push-ups in gym class long ago. I additionally recalled a quote from

Frederick Douglass that Coach once recited to me: "If there is no struggle, there is no progress." I struggled on and gradually made progress as the pain in my hip slowly subsided, then disappeared.

More importantly, the bone graft between my vertebrae fused successfully. When my gifted neurosurgeon Dr. Moustapha Abou-Samra, a veteran marathoner himself who understood my love for the sport, finally gave me the go-ahead to resume running I grabbed hold as if it were a life preserver in a choppy ocean. Dr. Abou-Samra said I could begin with *one* mile when I felt up to it; on July 7, 2003, I went on my first run in more than five months – *three* gingerly, slow, wonderful miles. An old friend was back in my life.

As I write this a decade later, I have run at least three miles every single day since.

On July 6, 2013, I celebrated a happy anniversary. Too, I marked a polar one. Dr. Freud would surely argue the two are related. And while this did not occur to me for quite some time, it now seems obvious and undeniable.

First, the celebratory anniversary. Or, as the United States Running Streak Association – yes, there is such a thing – terms it, "streakiversary." With a satisfying twelve-mile effort on July 6 my consecutive-day running streak (with an average of 8.6 miles daily over the span) reached ten years – or 3,653 days in a row thanks to three leap years.

If this strikes you as silly or insane, you are probably right on both counts. But according to the USRSA, which requires a minimum of a one-mile run per day, on my ten-year date there were one-hundred-and-fifty-two runners certifiably crazier than me – including eight in the "Legends" category with streaks surpassing 40 years!

I did not set out to become a "streaker." As a person caught red-handed in a love affair or addiction – and a running streak is no doubt a little of both – might guiltily explain: "It just happened." It happened in response to a life-changing event. Early on I believed this tragic catalyst was my being hit by the speeding drunk driver. Thus each run gave me a daily dose of empowerment over my physical losses.

Like a U.S. postal worker, I have not been detoured by rain nor sleet nor snow – nor falling ash from Southern California wildfires. I have run through injury and illness and after a late-night ambulance ride to the Emergency Room with a gallbladder attack whose symptoms mimicked a cardiac scare. When a battery of exams, including a treadmill stress test, came back with a clean bill of health I promptly laced up my Nikes and went on a three-mile run to extend The Streak – much to Lisa's concern and protest.

I have run at all hours insane or inconvenient to accommodate family plans, work schedules, time zones and even the International Date Line. Hopping off a plane in London, I kept The Streak alive by running three miles in the airport terminal at eleven p.m., causing one bemused Englishman to holler: "Hey, bloke! You must be a Yank 'cause you're bloody crazy!"

Perhaps. Although psychoanalysis might reveal something different at play. Indeed, while I did not realize it for a full year, it now seems beyond coincidence that my streak began on July 7, 2003. That was the due date of Lisa's and my third child.

A baby lost to miscarriage. Was the birth of The Streak a subconscious response to death?

The pregnancy had been a surprise, a wonderful one, and because my wife was forty-four, of high-risk. After Lisa made it safely into the second trimester we finally exhaled, allowing ourselves to get fully excited.

Then the heartbreak of no heartbeat.

It is likely a self-protective mechanism to try to rationalize a miscarriage as "being for the best because something was terribly wrong." Doctors, family and friends offer similar words of solace. And maybe the mind buys into this, but the heart does not.

We had chosen not to know the gender, perhaps another grasp at self-protection. Again, the heart has its own mind. A few years later my Lisa had a powerful dream in which she watched a child on a playground swing. The

110

girl, the same age our child would have then been, was happy. Rather than being overwhelmed with renewed grief, Lisa felt comforted.

I had no similar night vision.

However, over the years I have had many a daydream on runs while looking at kids – girls and boys – who are about the same age as my streak and thinking: That's how old our child would now be.

And then out of the blue in early July 2013, I had my own powerful sleep dream three nights in a row. Surely it was influenced by Lisa's dream from six years past, as well as by the approach of my ten-year streakiversary and hence the 2003 summer birthday that never was. In my dream I am running on the San Buenaventura State Beach bike path with a view of the gorgeous Pacific Ocean, one of my all-time very favorite routes. I am running alongside a child about age ten.

She is smiling and happy.

I think of her often now when I extend The Streak, my eyes sometimes salty as the sea.

Nine

The Streak

"The best competition I have is against myself to become better."
– John Wooden

Δ

My passion for distance running began in college as conditioning for the UC Santa Barbara tennis team, and then as a substitute for tennis after a back injury ended my competitive days swinging a racket. My senior year at UCSB I ran my first marathon and was smitten. After graduation I annually ran more than two thousand miles, year after year, and took this healthy physical release for granted. No longer. After long-distance running had been temporarily taken away from me – and I faced the realization my life had almost been taken – I came to see running as a precious gift.

Don't let what you cannot do interfere with what you can do. While I do not have control over the chronic pain in my neck, left shoulder, and left hand and fingers, I can control my decision to go for a run – just as Coach Wooden dedicated himself to taking a therapeutic daily walk following his heart attack at age sixty-two. Moreover, the endorphins released during exercise combined with the metronomic rhythm of running itself seems to relax and sooth my neck and shoulder.

Sometimes during a long run or race when fatigue and pain mount, I reach down and touch my right hipbone. Specifically, I use my index and middle fingers to feel the deep, smooth groove along the sharp iliac crest where some bone is missing as a result of my graft surgery and disc fusion. As I do this I often think of Coach's silver cross and a couplet from the poem "The Cross In My Pocket": *It reminds me, too, to be thankful / for my blessings day by day.*

Coach gives me further motivation through his own wise poetic words: "There is a choice you have to make in everything you do. And you must always keep in mind, the choices you make – make you." I make the choice to be a runner each day.

As a consequence of the drunk driver, I faced a more difficult choice. The long commute to press boxes in Los Angeles considerably aggravated the chronic discomfort in my neck, shoulder and left hand. Hunching over my laptop during deadline pressure, trying to be quick without hurrying but having no time for a rest break to stretch my inflamed neck, made matters unbearable. In truth the choice was made for me: I had to leave my dream job as a sports columnist.

This only made my running habit all the more important – it kept the drunk driver from robbing even more from me. Lacing up my shoes each day became a positive choice that empowered me mentally as well as physically: if I could run each day, then surely I could also still write. The opening stanza from another of Coach's favored poems, "Don't Quit" by an author whose name is lost to time, buoyed my resolve to press on:

> *When things go wrong as they sometimes will,*
> *When the road you're trudging seems all uphill,*
>
> *When the funds are low and the debts are high,*
> *And you want to smile, but you have to sigh,*
>
> *When care is pressing you down a bit –*
> *Rest if you must, but don't you quit.*

While I was leaving behind the press box and long commutes, I was not quitting my writing career. I just needed to change my venue. By becoming a freelancer I was able break up my writing into one-hour sessions, each followed by a short rest break for my neck and hand before returning to the keyboard.

Things turn out best for those who make the best of the way things turn out. As a freelance writer unchained by a rigid schedule I was able to visit Dallas at college for lunch almost once a week her entire four years at the University of Southern California. Regularly seeing Greg at USC and attending all but one of his cross-country and track meets as a Trojan similarly would have been impossible had I remained a newspaper sports columnist.

Unless I had been forced to leave the newspaper business, I would have likely pursued my columnist career at a growing expense to family. Instead, I took on new challenges – such as writing this book. And, in time, I returned to my old newspaper, *The Ventura County Star*; not in sports, but as a general interest columnist on the Op-Ed page each Saturday, a new forum that has been both stimulating and rewarding.

In short, I took charge of my circumstances. And as Coach emphasized, this is essential to making the best of our circumstances. This, in turn, is necessary to becoming the best we are capable of becoming.

Lisa is a dedicated runner herself, completing numerous marathons, but when I get out of a sickbed to log another three miles or rise at three a.m. to run before a long travel day to keep The Streak alive, she rolls her eyes and shakes her head – and sometimes cannot suppress a smile.

I have run more marathons post neck surgery than

before it. And, excluding my very first marathon at age twenty-one when I broke three hours (2:58), my fastest times have come *after* the car crash, including a post-college personal record of 3:11 at age forty-nine. Yes, things do turn out best for those who make the best of the way things turn out.

When someone learns about my streak, they invariably ask some variation of: "How in the world can you do that?" My reply is that running one-hundred days in a row is actually easier than running ninety-nine days out of one-hundred; running 365 days in a row is easier than running 360 out 365 days; and thus by extrapolation running every day for nearly 4,000 consecutive days is in some ways easier than taking a few days off because there is no decision to wrestle with daily.

As the great Czech distance runner Emil Zatopek, who remarkably won gold medals in the marathon *and* 10,000 meters *and* 5,000 meters in the 1952 Helsinki Olympics, once wisely noted: "When a person trains once, nothing happens. When a person forces himself to do a thing one-hundred times then he certainly has developed in more ways than physical. Is it raining? That doesn't matter. Am I tired? That doesn't matter either. The willpower is no longer a problem."

And so it is with me, a non-Olympian. There is no longer a question of whether I will run today: I simply *will*.

It does not matter if it is raining or I am tired. My willpower is no longer a problem. Running has become as much a part of my daily routine as brushing my teeth and showering and eating. I awaken each morning knowing that running will be part of making today my masterpiece.

The Streak has not been a purely selfish endeavor. Part of the motivation has been to set a positive example for Dallas and Greg by putting some of Coach's wisdom into action. Just as The Streak is built one day, and one run, at a time, so is any personal masterpiece – be it creating a painting, writing a book, finishing a marathon, earning good grades, forming a charitable foundation, fostering a friendship, nurturing a loving marriage – built step by step. One stroke at the easel, one typed word on a keyboard, one lap around the track, one study session, one hour volunteering, one kind deed, one hug at a time we make our mark. By making today your masterpiece, and then stringing the days together like pearls on a necklace into your own streak, you create a masterpiece of a life.

Coach's lesson in the value of *balance* has been paramount in The Streak. I surely could not have run every day for more than a decade had I stubbornly insisted on a daily minimum of ten miles or demanded from myself a hard effort each outing. However, by allowing as few as three miles to occasionally suffice, by often running easily and slowly, the balanced efforts kept me from wearing down physically and mentally. And so it is true in other pursuits: short, easy sessions of just ten or fifteen minutes writing or painting or studying can add up impressively, especially when balanced with longer work sessions.

To be certain, just as there are days I want to avoid planting my butt in a chair in front of my computer keyboard, there are days I do not want to run. But it is precisely when I am sick or the weather is nasty, or my neck pain is flaring up after too many hours at the typewriter the previous day, that the accomplishment and self-satisfaction is most authentic. As Coach put it: "Earn the right to be proud and confident. Goals achieved with little effort are seldom worthwhile or lasting." Days containing adversity are the days when these rewards are most possible.

While I certainly do feel a sense of pride in The Streak, I generally only add up its length each January 1 and again on its anniversary each July 6. After all, Coach advised: "Don't let yesterday take up too much of today." Nor do I look ahead and focus on extending The Streak to the next yearly figure or upcoming hundred-day or thousand-day milestone. It is more important to keep in mind a famous quote by Cervantes, author of *Don Quixote*, who Coach liked very much, and repeated often: "The journey is better than the inn."

The journey of The Streak is fun and satisfying. I try to enjoy each run, each masterpiece day. Just as the day came for Coach Wooden when arthritic knees and hips forced him to cease his beloved morning walks, I know the day will arrive when my streak ends. Until then I want to savor these days, even days when my neck hurts or my back aches or my Achilles tendon is sore. One day when I cannot run, I will wish I could even if only at a slow gingerly shuffle.

I think The Streak can serve as a metaphor for many things in life – even for life itself. The day will come when my streak of consecutive days living will come to an end, too. In the meantime, today I will once more smooth my socks with care and lace up my running shoes while being sure to tie the double-knot directly over an eyelet just as Coach taught me long ago.

Ten

No Deposit, No Return

———

"Good things take time, as they should. We shouldn't expect good things to happen overnight. Actually, getting something too easily or too soon can cheapen the outcome."

– John Wooden

Δ

Often during the course of my running streak, especially on those rare days I do not feel like lacing on my shoes and heading out the front door, I have think of swimming great John Naber and a story he shared with me during an interview – and which I later shared with Coach, who enjoyed it very much.

Bruce Jenner, the 1976 Olympic decathlon champion, claimed with tongue in cheek (and a handsome endorsement check in the bank) that he won the gold medal because he ate his Wheaties. Actually, Jenner told me more truthfully, "A bowl of Wheaties *and* ten-thousand hours of hard work will give you everything you want."

John Naber, meanwhile, has credited his Olympic glory – four gold medals won in four world-record times and one silver medal – in those same 1976 Montreal Summer Olympic Games to drinking root beer. Specifically, a bottle of root beer he had when he was eleven years old. He is serious. It seems that while pausing between gulps of that caramel-colored carbonated magic potion, young John noticed the raised letters on the bottleneck: *No Deposit, No Return.*

This became Naber's personal mantra, his creed reminding him that without the Deposit of hard work there is no Return of improvement and success. Furthermore, he reasoned, a lot of Deposit would mean a lot of Return.

And so John dedicated himself to rising before the crack of dawn at 5:30 nearly every morning thereafter, diving into a cold swimming pool and making a deposit of two hours of hard work *before* school. After his classes he would deposit two more hours of hard work in the pool. In total he swam four hours a day, six days a week, year after year after year.

Coach Wooden warned, "Never mistake activity for achievement" and Ernest Hemingway echoed, "Never confuse movement with action." Naber proved this advice sound: the swimmer's daily deposit of action added up to great achievement. Indeed, like compound interest in a savings account, his deposits grew and multiplied.

Eventually the deposits of sweat and effort added up to the equivalent of swimming around the earth's equator. Twice!

It also added up to Olympic glory in the Montreal chlorine, becoming the first man to break the two-minute barrier in the 200-meter backstroke, and for good measure the 1977 Sullivan Award as America's Most Outstanding Athlete.

"Olympic champions are not extraordinary people," Naber told me. "We are ordinary people who accomplish extraordinary things in something that mattered to us. If we believe Olympic champions are not extraordinary, and if we believe we are at least ordinary, then we can all accomplish great things in our lives."

Of course, accomplishing great things in our lives requires dedication and effort. *No Deposit, No Return.* In other words, a bottle of root beer and ten-thousand hours of hard work will give you everything you want.

Or, as Coach Wooden put it in verse:

> *Remember this your lifetime through:*
> *Tomorrow there will be more to do.*
>
> *And failure waits for all who stay*
> *With some success made yesterday.*
>
> *Tomorrow you must try once more,*
> *And even harder than before.*

Here is a second story about John Naber that also made Wooden smile approvingly, for it exemplified Coach's own beliefs in sportsmanship being more valuable than gold and that "the true test of a man's character is what he does when no one is watching."

As mentioned, at the tender age of twenty Naber put his historic stamp on the 1976 Summer Olympic Games. His greatest performance, however, may not have come in the Montreal pool. It may not have even resulted in an Olympic gold medal or a world record.

Naber's greatest performance arguably came three years earlier in the U.S. Trials for the 1973 World Championships. The situation was this: if John wins the race at hand, he not only makes the team individually but also earns a spot as the backstroke leg on the American relay squad.

Naber finished first. A glorious victory.

But wait. Hold the celebration.

"On the turn there was a question if I had a legal touch," Naber recalled decades later. "My coach told me it was my word versus the judge's. He told me we could fight it – and win it."

Understand, winning the appeal would secure Naber a trip to the World Championships where he would have a chance to win two medals.

"It was a no-brainer," Naber continued matter-of-factly of the decision he faced. He paused, and then added surprisingly and honestly: "I *did* miss the turn."

And so, in turn, he did miss going to the World Championships after refusing to appeal the lane judge's call.

"I don't regret it," this cross between a merman and Boy Scout continued. "It was the right thing to do."

Naber knows winning isn't everything.

"The joy of achievement is its own reward," Naber insisted, and correctly. "I haven't seen my Olympic gold medals in years – they're in a museum in Los Angeles. I don't care to see them. To me the worth is not in *having* a gold medal, but in *earning* the gold medal. I relive the memories of touching the wall first, all the time."

A greater golden highlight might be reliving the memory of the time John Naber touched the wall first, but unfairly – and had the character to admit it.

Eleven

Orange Peels

———

"Little things make big things happen."
– John Wooden

Δ

Coach Wooden was a constant example of doing the right thing, the kind thing, the good thing. Often it was a little and simple thing.

For example, on our first shared morning walk I felt slightly embarrassed when he abruptly stopped, stepped behind me and across the sidewalk, and then bent down to pick up a discarded hamburger wrapper. I had not seen it, so intent was my focus on listening to Coach's every syllable, though to be honest I doubt I would have stopped and interrupted our walk to pick it up even had I spotted it.

A couple more times Coach contributed to the cleanup of his neighborhood that morning – "Pick up your own orange peels," he liked to say – and, of course, I now followed his example and likewise picked up a couple pieces of litter myself. The power of his simple example lasted well beyond that morning. Ever since I have tried to be more aware of "orange peels" and pick up litter I see in my daily life.

After Coach passed away, I naturally reminisced a lot about our walks – and the image of him picking up wrappers and cans inspired me as never before. Just as he was a caretaker for the four-and-a-half-mile route he walked daily, I decided to dedicate myself to beautifying a favored running route near my home.

I could have chosen to clean it up with one or two weekends of concentrated effort. Instead, I recalled Coach's example and maxim "Little things make big things happen." It echoed a story of the bamboo fields that golfing legend Chi Chi Rodriguez once told me.

"When I was a young boy we had a little field that was overgrown with bamboo trees," Rodriguez recalled of his childhood in Puerto Rico. "My father wanted to plant corn, but clearing the bamboo would have taken a month. He didn't have the time because of his job.

"So every night when he came home from work, my father would cut down a single piece of bamboo."

Chi Chi paused, and then emphasized: "Just one piece."

Another pause. And a smile.

"The very next spring, we had corn on our dinner table."

A longer pause. And a wider smile.

"The lesson is that nothing is impossible," continued Rodriquez, who is affectionately called "Uncle Chi Chi" by the underprivileged students at the Chi Chi Rodriguez Youth Foundation he founded in Clearwater, Florida. "We dress the kids, we feed them, we teach them manners. And we give them self-esteem. You can't be a success without self-esteem."

Or without hard work.

"My father always told me that if a man pays you five dollars to do a job, you give him eight dollars worth of work," Chi Chi further related. "That way you'll feel good about yourself – and you'll have more work the next day. I tell the students the bamboo story because to me it's the secret to success. If you really want something and you set your mind to it and work hard enough, one by one, little by little, miracles happen."

In Coach's honor I set my mind to clearing my own bamboo field, so to speak, little by little. Truth is, if I stopped to pick up all the litter and trash I spotted on my eight-mile and twelve-mile and even longer runs, I would need to push a jogging stroller if not a wheelbarrow. Instead, I decided to dedicate my efforts to a one-mile stretch near my home. Specifically, it is busy two-lane road with a wide dirt berm on the south side where it borders a lemon orchard. While this stretch smells citrusy wonderful during picking season, it has also become a dumpsite of sorts.

This picturesque path-turned-eyesore had saddened me for a long time and it chagrins me to admit I routinely ran along it for nearly a decade before finally being motivated to take action. Thinking of Coach Wooden's example I was also reminded of a "Keep America Beautiful" public announcement TV commercial from my youth. The spot, created in 1971 by the Ad Council, featured a stoic Native American chief played by actor Iron Eyes Cody with one lonely teardrop slowly rolling down his deeply lined face as he sees litter being tossed out the window of a passing car.

At the height of the campaign, "Keep America Beautiful" was receiving about two thousand letters a month from people seeking to join local chapters. The end result was a grassroots effort that restored a measure of beauty across America by reducing litter by as much as eighty-eight percent in three hundred communities throughout thirty-eight states.

Four decades later, I think Iron Eyes would be openly sobbing. According to recent statistics, fifty-one billion pieces of litter land on American roadways each year – that's 6,729 items per mile! Moreover, the life span of litter is staggering: it is estimated an aluminum can takes two hundred years to decompose; plastic six-pack rings, four hundred and fifty years; a glass bottle, one million years. Even a cigarette butt takes one to five years to decompose.

Deciding to make America a little more beautiful along a one-mile stretch of road in Southern California and give Iron Eyes Cody's character a small reason to smile was the easy part. Doing so proved to be much more of a Sisyphean challenge than I had anticipated: no sooner would I make three steps of progress forward when newly tossed litter would set me back two steps.

I have numerous running routes of various distances and directions mapped from my house but for nearly a year, regardless of which one I chose to take on any given day, I made certain to circle around so that the one-mile stretch was included at the finish. This way I made daily progress and did not have to carry the trash I picked up for my entire run. It was also a nice way to finish a workout on a positive note.

One handful at a time I tackled the routine litter first: fast-food bags and paper wrappers; soda cans and beer bottles; and plastic grocery bags which came in handy for carrying more trash than usual. Sometimes I brought along a plastic spoon and focused on scooping up disgusting cigarette butts, and worse, into a plastic bag.

Next I went after other small stuff like DVDs and CDs; batteries and books; an alarm clock and a couple of dead cell phones; clothes and shoes; Barbie dolls with broken limbs and stuffed animals in need of sutures; wrenches and screwdrivers and saw blades; even a football helmet that I wore home while running and a wallet with money still in it that I was able to return to its owner.

I did not ignore the bigger stuff – such as a television, stereos, a drum set, a car muffler, and a bike frame – but rather took a different approach. For example, the heavy and cumbersome TV was tackled by carrying it about twenty yards closer to my home each day. This way I lessened the risk of tweaking a back muscle or hamstring while also minimizing the interruption to my run. Following the bamboo field example, in a matter of a few weeks I got the TV home and then drove it to the e-waste recycling center.

Some stuff was simply too big and too heavy to lug home even incrementally. A loveseat, for example, I struggled just to move ten yards up to the side of the road from its resting site halfway down an embankment sloping to the orchard. However, only days later I was able to flag down a trash truck in the convoy that frequents the road. After I explained my project they happily and helpfully hauled it away.

Too, there have been a couple of road-kill coyotes and one full-grown hog that must have caused major fender damage; for these I phoned Animal Control.

All told, I have cleaned up most everything from A to Z but the kitchen sink – I am barely exaggerating as I did clear away a bathroom sink!

Cleaning up my unofficial "Adopt A Highway" one-mile stretch of roadway is a Sisyphean task much like painting the Golden Gate Bridge – when you finish the chore by reaching one end it is time to start anew at the other. Still, it is a rewarding undertaking. When I pick up other people's "orange peels" – on a run or walking around town – I like to imagine Coach Wooden smiling approvingly.

I also picture a pleased Iron Eyes Cody, now a recreational runner in my mind's eye, with sweat from a good workout rolling down his cheek instead of a teardrop.

Twelve

The Self-Esteem Ape

"Never forget how special you are."
– John Wooden,
speaking with Dallas and Greg

Δ

In extension of his friendship, the greatest gift Coach Wooden gave me was the act of love he showed by inviting Dallas and Greg over to his home for an afternoon visit.

It was August of 1997. Dallas was ten and Greg not yet eight. The teacher-philosopher-author-humanitarian-poet-great-grandfather, and yes, legendary coach, came walking around the outside corner. He was moving much more slowly than when I first joined him on his morning walk a full decade earlier. Still, he approached us moving steadily – and perhaps a little stubbornly too – without aid of a cane despite having an artificial hip and an ailing knee that his doctors told him needed total replacement.

Coach could have avoided the uncomfortable, if not even slightly painful, walk by "buzzing" us in through the locked gate surrounding the condominium complex, but that would not have been as polite as a personal welcome. Make no mistake, it would pain John Wooden more to be thought of as impolite than to suffer a small measure of physical ache. Indeed, he would prefer to have been thought of as a gentleman than as the greatest basketball coach who ever lived. He was, of course, both.

On several occasions Coach had graciously extended an open invitation to me to bring Dallas and Greg for a visit. Frankly, I should have taken him up on the kind offer much sooner than I did; in hindsight, however, I am actually thankful I waited until Dallas and Greg were old enough to truly take it all in and fully appreciate it and forever remember it. While they had not yet met in person, Coach knew all about them both from our talks and visits and they in turn had been raised hearing Wooden-ism sayings and stories.

Leading the three of us back inside his immaculate-but-unpretentious home, the first thing Coach did was excuse himself to retrieve something from a shelf in the living room. One of his ten NCAA national championship trophies? A Coach of the Year or Hall of Fame plaque? Perhaps a replica trophy of the John R. Wooden Award that is presented annually to the most outstanding college basketball player of the year? Or maybe he was getting down one of the many humanitarian awards that have him sharing august company with such notables as Mother Teresa, Jimmy Carter, and Melinda Gates?

"Heavens sakes, no!" to borrow one of Wooden's favorite phrases of exasperation, he was not fetching any of those. Besides, most of that impressive memorabilia was modestly hidden away in his study.

John Wooden, the famous Wizard of Westwood, turned around and was holding . . .

. . . a small, stuffed gorilla about the size of a teddy bear. It was wearing a red vest with a matching bowtie. And the fancy anthropoid could talk.

"You're a genius!!!" the talking stuffed ape in the fancy red vest said enthusiastically, his words of praise meriting three exclamation marks at the least.

"Excellent thinking!!!" it continued.

"You're brilliant!!!"

"Grrrreat idea!!!"

"That's fabuuuulous!!!"

"That's awesome!!!"

"Outstanding!!!"

Greg and Dallas laughed, as did I. Wooden smiled at them and then glanced at me with a knowing wink. What appeared to be a toy to others, The Greatest Basketball Coach Who Ever Lived saw as a teaching tool.

"This is The Self-Esteem Ape," Coach explained softly and warmly as he cradled the stuffed animal given to him by his daughter Nan. "When our self-esteem is a little low, we all need to be picked up a little."

John Wooden was The Self-Esteem Wizard.

The photograph I snapped that afternoon of my young children sitting on Coach's lap reveals how comfortable they felt in his company from the start. The fact that Dallas and Greg have each taken a framed print of the picture with them to every college dorm room and apartment they have lived in since leaving home reveals how important the afternoon was to them. Indeed, both frequently cite it as one of the favorite days in their lives.

During the two-hour visit with Dallas and Greg, Coach talked about basketball for about five minutes and spent the rest of the time sharing stories about his children and grandchildren and great-grandchildren. About Nellie. About his idols Abraham Lincoln ("There is nothing stronger than gentleness") and Mother Teresa ("If you can't feed a hundred people, feed just one"). About his famous Pyramid of Success and his father Joshua's *Two Sets of Threes*:

> *Don't whine. Don't complain. Don't make excuses.*
> *Never lie. Never cheat. Never steal.*

Escorting his three visitors back out to the front gate at the conclusion of the rose-petal-pressed-in-ascrapbook-like afternoon, Coach Wooden added a fourth *Never*:

"Never forget," the Self-Esteem Wizard told Dallas and Greg, "how special you are."

Δ

Coach's good-bye words to Dallas and Greg remind me of the advice I heard Sparky Anderson share when he was the commencement speaker at Dorsey High School in Los Angeles.

"I would say to you that I'm very proud of you," the Dorsey Class of 1963 graduate began, touching on the theme of the previous orators while looking around at the mosaic of faces forming Dorsey's Class of 2001. "But everyone says that. I don't want it that way. I want *you* to be proud of yourselves. I want *you* to look in the mirror and be proud of the person you see. Don't look in the mirror and have it tell you how bad you are.

"There are two things I want you to do," continued Sparky, wearing a gray suit, red tie, white shirt and whiter hair. "I want you to go to bed at night and say this prayer: 'I am the most precious person on Earth.' And then repeat it when you wake up each morning."

Dorsey High's graduating class collectively earned more than $1.5 million in various scholarships and grants, with members going on to universities not only throughout California but across the nation. Sparky – who passed away on November 4, 2010, five months to the day after Coach Wooden – never went to college. But make no mistake, he had a sheepskin from the University of Life with a Ph.D. in wisdom.

"It's so important to be proud," Sparky emphasized to the graduating students, and who could be more of an expert on the subject? After all, he was the first manager to win World Series championships in both the National League (Cincinnati Reds in 1975 and '76) and American League (Detroit Tigers in 1984) and was the third-winningest manager in history with 2,194 career victories before retiring in 1995.

Yet Sparky sincerely insisted, echoing Coach Wooden's own feelings, that he was more proud of raising three children into fine adults and being a doting grandfather fourteen times over than he was of any professional honor, even his induction into the Baseball Hall of Fame.

You see, Sparky never mistook statistics and salaries, nor championships and trophies, for true success.

"The word *success* – I wish they'd take it out of the dictionary," Sparky told the Class of '01. "Today, *success* has come to mean how much money you have; how big of a house; how fancy of a car you drive."

He shook his head disapprovingly, and then set the matter straight: "That's not success."

It was not lip service. This was a man who earned a seven-figure annual salary as a famous manager, yet lived in the same modest home in Thousand Oaks, California, for the last three decades of his life. Also like Wooden he rarely traded in his old car for a newer model – and kept his friends even longer.

"Success is what kind of a human being you are," Sparky continued to the graduating teens. "It is what I do as a person, how I act as a person, that is important. When they put you in that box at the end of your life, if you were a good person you will have been successful."

Had he been in attendance that afternoon, John Wooden would have surely stood and applauded Sparky's commencement address. Additionally, Coach likely would have told each student he met afterward: "Never forget how special you are."

Thirteen

Lunchbox Notes

———

"Happiness begins where selfishness ends."
– John Wooden

Δ

Long before their priceless afternoon visit with Coach Wooden, I made a daily habit of writing notes such as "Have a great day!" or "Good luck on your spelling test!" or "I miss you lots!" on paper napkins and putting them inside Dallas's Little Mermaid lunchbox and Greg's Power Rangers lunchbox. Sometimes I would add a pearl from Coach such as "Be quick, but don't hurry" (which was a great reminder before a spelling test) or "Happiness begins where selfishness ends" and so on.

After they met Coach, I made sure to *always* include a Wooden-ism. The previously mentioned Seven-Point Creed that was given to "Johnny" when he was 12 years old by his father Joshua became a frequent go-to jotting, one line at a time:

Be true to yourself.
Make each day your masterpiece.
Help others.
Drink deeply from good books.
Make friendship a fine art.
Build shelter against a rainy day.
Pray for guidance and give thanks for your blessings every day.

It was not long before Dallas and Greg were reciting Wooden-isms back to me. We discussed these sayings at the dinner table. We also talked about the Pyramid of Success and, of course, Wooden's personal definition of success. In my heart of hearts I know these notes and conversations made a deep and lasting impact. Dallas and Greg became young students of Coach Wooden and put his teachings into practice.

Here is but one memorable early example of when Dallas exemplified "Help others" and "Make friendship a fine art" from the Seven-Point Creed. She was in third grade and her teacher, Mrs. Ford, asked to speak with me after class one day. I was a little surprised because Dallas has always been an excellent student, but it wasn't schoolwork her teacher wanted to discuss.

"We have a new student in class," Mrs. Ford explained, "and it's never easy to come to a new school in the middle of the school year. But your daughter has gone out of her way to make Julie feel welcome. The very first day, Dallas befriended Julie in class. She even invited Julie to sit with her and her friends at lunch and has done so every day since."

I smiled, but Mrs. Ford sensed I was not as impressed as she felt I should be. "You don't understand how rare such kindness is, at her age or any age," she rejoined. "And the other kids have slowly followed Dallas' example."

A short while later, Mrs. Ford again called me into her classroom after school let out. Again she wanted to share an act of kindness by Dallas. It seems each week a student who had done something special in class – read the most pages, aced a spelling test, that sort of thing – was awarded a prize. For the third week in a row, the winner was Dallas.

And for the second week in a row Dallas had privately told Mrs. Ford that it wasn't right for her to get another prize and to please award it to another student who had not yet been honored.

"Dallas is so kind," Mrs. Ford said. "She never wants anyone to feel left out. You must have done something very special in raising her."

While Lisa and I would surely like to take full credit, in truth I think Coach Wooden deserves an assist.

Here is a similar example exhibited by Greg when he was a senior in high school. Rather than tell the story, I will share two handwritten notes from a fellow student in Greg's Advanced Placement Art Class and personally delivered on Senior Night 2005. The first was given to Lisa and me; the second to Greg.

Dear Mrs. & Mr. Woodburn,

I doubt you have heard of me and I have not had the pleasure of meeting you. However, I'd just like to say that your son Greg is the nicest ("young man" is scratched out) *person I have ever met. He helped me transform from a dark mess of a writer who hated himself into a dark writer who finally feels he is worth something.*

Your son is truly amazing. You see, a lot of my poetry was about my own self-loathing. Until your son suggested I change the words from hate, to love. I've never been told that.

Your son saved my life that day. And though I thank him daily in my thoughts, I'd like to thank you for raising such an amazing man. You should be proud of him. Thank you for your time.

– Scott

Dear Mr. Greg Woodburn,

Let's see, now, what can I say about you that hasn't been said already. Probably nothing. Greg, I just wanted to say thank you

*for saving my life. You are truly among the
most amazing people that have ever, will, and
currently walk the Earth.*

*I haven't the faintest clue as to how
you do it, but you are just this phenomenal
being. I wish there were more people like you. I
can tell when people are full of it. And when
they're not. You are of the few who I have felt to
be sincere. Thank you. Generally when people
talk, they sound like they've got their heads in
their tucus. You captivate me when you speak.
You are greatness, sir. Never forget that. Please
stay as pure as you are today.*

*If you ever need anything, I'm there in
a heartbeat. I'd take a bullet for you man. Stay
Platinum. And I'll see you when we're on top.
Love you man.*

– Scott

Δ

Both Dallas and Greg have been fortunate to receive the
prestigious national Jefferson Award for Public Service and
the Congressional Award Gold Medal, among other
esteemed honors – but the above heartfelt words from a
fellow student and from a teacher are laurels valued just as
dearly. Such compliments are evidence that Dallas and
Greg have put the Seven-Point Creed into daily practice.

Coach's sayings and maxims also inspired Greg to
begin keeping a journal with his own musings, such as:

Patience is a bitter seed but a sweet fruit.

The companions you walk with, as much as the steps you take, define your journey.

Do not be pushed by your fears; be led by your dreams.

Strive, strive, strive, and you will achieve; dedication can plug many gaps.

You cannot take an elevator to the top of a mountain.

The happiest paintbrushes are the worn-through ones.

Love is both the sculptor and the marble.

Giving compliments does a lot more good than taking out the trash, and should thus be done more than once a week.

You never know the new friends you can make when you smile and listen.

Laughter is human sunlight.

A gentle touch and a kind word are passing, but what each conveys remains.

Giving becomes real when it becomes personal.

Asking for help is not weakness, just as rain is not bad weather.

A small step taken today gets you further than promising to take a big step tomorrow.

Discipline makes the details, and details make the difference.

*Time allows us to grow. Time allows us to love. And what is
more, time allows our love to grow.*

Don't let worry delay enjoyment of the day.

*Age depends on attitude: worry ages us, while wonder makes us
young.*

The quickest, surest way to impoverish yourself is through hate.

Let compassion *be your* compass.

Chasing dreams will get you further than chasing dollars.

Follow your principles, not a road map.

*If life always went according to plan, it wouldn't turn out for the
best.*

*You are never too big to do the little things, and you are never so
little that you can't do big things.*

The quickest way to the heart is through a helping hand.

*Saying "You're welcome" is as important as saying "Thank
you."*

Δ

A number of Greg's journal entries remind me of a story
Magic Johnson shared with me.

Magic, an NBA Hall of Famer with 10,141 career

assists, says his mother Christine is the greatest and most selfless assist-maker he has ever seen. Understand, he was not talking about no-look assists. Or behind-the-back assists. Or thread-the-needle bounce-pass assists.

Rather assists that lead to the happiness of others, not to two points. More along the lines of baskets of fruit for the hungry, not baskets at the end of a fastbreak. Assists in the form of a helping hand; the kind of assists that Wooden most admired.

"My mom would give the shirt off her back if someone needed it," Magic told me. "She'd give her shoes and her last piece of bread. She'd give everything to others. She'd rather others have what they need – that makes her happy. That's the way she still is."

Like mother, like son. Though it was not always that way – on the court and off it.

"Basketball-wise, I wasn't always unselfish either," Magic confessed. "Basketball-wise, my unselfishness developed because I wanted to win.

"I used to dominate in elementary school so much the parents would get upset," the Lakers legend explained. "I played CYO ball when I was eight, nine, ten years old and there were times my team would score fifteen baskets and I would score thirteen of them. We'd win and I'd be real happy, but the other kids' parents would be unhappy because their kids weren't getting any points.

"As I got older, maybe twelve, I realized I could be happy and make the other guys happy too. I decided to help the other kids score. I figured they'd be happy they scored and we'd win which would make me happy."

Magic had embraced these two Wooden adages: *It is amazing how much can be accomplished if no one cares who gets the credit* and *It takes ten hands to put the ball in the basket.*

"So you see, I used to be a scorer when I was little," Magic added. "I came to see the other side. It's like Christmas – the older you get, the more you realize that giving can make you happy."

Off the court, Christine taught her young son Earvin – known back then as "Junior" or "June Bug" in their Lansing, Michigan neighborhood – the magic of giving.

"My mom would keep giving and giving," shared Magic. "Somebody in the neighborhood is sick and can't cook dinner? My mom would cook and take them dinner until they got well. She'd help them with everything until they got better."

Her caring help was not limited to the sick.

"She'd cut the lawn for four or five neighbors and shovel four driveways in the winter too because they were too old to," Magic marveled. "My mom would get over there and do it."

Or else have Junior do it.

"They gonna pay me?" Magic the man recalls Earvin the boy replying. "No? Then I'm not gonna do it."

Wrong.

"Boom, I had to do it anyway," Magic resumed, laughing. "She'd just give everything, even lend her kids.

"I learned about giving from her," continued Magic, who won five NBA championships during his storied career and also won the league's prestigious Walter Kennedy Citizenship Award for his community efforts. Indeed, the 1992 Olympic gold medalist with a gilded heart to match makes the initials of his three league MVP awards stand for Most Valuable Philanthropist, noting: "Now, I *have* to do it. I just *have* to."

That includes raising millions of dollars annually for a wide range of charities.

"Raising money and helping others is something I *have* to do," Magic repeated, smiling. "My life is built around giving now. I love to give and give back. That's what living and life is all about – giving."

Credit that attitude to the biggest assist that came from Magic Mom. And, as Coach Wooden always insisted of his players after they scored a basket, Magic pointed an appreciative finger of acknowledgement at the person who passed it along to him.

Fourteen

Soaring Eagles

"Don't measure yourself by what you've accomplished,
but rather by what you should have accomplished
with your abilities."

– John Wooden

Δ

You are surely familiar with the story about The Little
Engine That Could. Well, this story is about The Little Boy
Who Could.

His name was Colin. Age eight. Second-grader with
short bangs, thick glasses and a lazy right eye. Little guy,
big smile. His mountain to chug-chug-chug up was the
American Youth Soccer Association season.

Confession. As the head coach of my son's AYSO
Golden Eagles, at our very first practice I knew Colin was
the least-talented player on the team. It was a tipoff when
he tripped over his own feet and fell down during the
warm-up jog before he even tried to kick a ball. He made

someone with two left feet look like a "Dancing With The Stars" champion by comparison.

I would like to tell you that thanks to my wonderful coaching Colin magically metamorphosed from an ugly duckling into a graceful swan; a soaring Golden Eagle, if you will. That he scored a hat trick with three goals in one game and a dozen goals over the entire season. I would like to tell you all of that, but I cannot. He did not.

No, Colin did not figuratively fly or literally score a single goal. All the same, I can tell you this: he soared the highest and scored the biggest goal of all – he kept chugging up the mountain.

I think I can, I think I can. The Little Boy Who Could. Or, at least, Who Never Stopped Trying – which, as John Wooden always pointed out, is a far greater thing. Colin was a role model for maximizing what one could accomplish with his or her abilities. Indeed, the AYSO season began shortly after Dallas and Greg had met and visited with Wooden, and I used Colin as a visible example of true success.

The Golden Eagles actually had two Colins. One had previously attended summer soccer camps and was terrifically coordinated and a superb player; the other had not and was neither. Talking about the two at the dinner table, I would avoid confusion by referring to them as "Star Colin" and "Little Colin."

But a funny thing happened along the season's journey. I noticed that no one's determination was bigger than Little Colin's. The other thirteen kids would race through the slalom course of small plastic orange cones, missing some along the way, but not Little Colin. Never Little Colin. Slowly, deliberately, he would dribble the soccer ball with left foot . . . right foot . . . left . . . right . . . through each and every cone, his eyes focused downward on the task, his tongue sticking out in total concentration, a giggle oftentimes rolling over his lips.

I think I can, I think I can.

There was more. Little Colin would play where he was instructed to play, be it at forward or midfielder or fullback. No small thing, this. Staying within the same ZIP Code of the assigned area on the field is more difficult than long division for first- and second-graders who are generally attracted to the soccer ball like bees to a hive. But Little Colin, bless him, did not fall into the "swarm ball" trap. I cannot say that about more than maybe three of his teammates.

And by no means did Little Colin just stand in his spot like a rooted tree. He displayed a nose for the ball. He surprisingly showed no fear getting into the thick of the mix. Without any speed to brag of, he would race to the ball and get in his fair share of kicks each game.

Which is not to say Little Colin became the best

player on the team, or even tenth best. But perhaps he did something much more remarkable and surely more admirable: he came closest to reaching his potential. He might have even surpassed it if such a thing is possible. Certainly this skinny, four-foot-two-inch Rocky Balboa in shin guards surpassed what I thought he could possibly accomplish.

"Don't measure yourself by what you have accomplished, but by what you should have accomplished with your ability," Coach Wooden said. By this measurement Little Colin stood tall. By this measurement he soared high. He also epitomized a stanza from "The Road Ahead," which Coach liked to recite: *Who can ask more of a man, than giving all within his span? / Giving all, it seems to me, is not so far from victory.*

Still, there was more about this boy who gave all within his span. Before one practice, Little Colin brought me a small gift-wrapped package. Inside was a huge piece of bubble gum. Another time he brought me a drawing he had made. Once, a poem. Always, he brought a smile to practice and in turn brought a smile to my face.

Fifteen years later, on a May morning in 2013, tears came to my face when I saw Colin's picture in a newspaper obituary. The Little Boy Who Could had become a remarkable young man. He joined the Navy as a corpsman and had recently returned from deployment in

Afghanistan. The kind boy who had given me small gifts before practices now dreamed of becoming a doctor after his stint in the service. The uncoordinated second-grader had matured into an athlete who completed a handful of triathlons and learned to surf. He also rode a motorcycle, an accident on which tragically claimed his life at age twenty-three.

I dug out the scrapbooks. But when I found the team picture Colin was not in it. Then I remembered: the day it was taken, Little Colin was absent because of yet another doctor's appointment. That is disappointing, of course, but the truth is it does not matter all that much to me. You see, besides my son, The Little Boy Who Could – and Did – is the one Golden Eagle I will never forget.

Δ

Here is another inspiring story of an eagle, one related to me by Olympic track legend Billy Mills.

One of thirteen children, Billy grew up on the Pine Ridge Reservation in South Dakota. The family's three-room house was so small and crowded that in the summer Billy would sleep outside under the stars.

"We were in poverty," Mills shared, "but I didn't know it. There was always food to eat."

And, more importantly: "We always had love."

A great deal of that love was lost when Billy was just seven years young and his mother died from cancer. After her death, however, a dream was born when Billy's father read him a book about the Olympic Games.

"It said, 'Olympians are chosen by the Gods,' " Mills remembers vividly. "That's when I first dreamed of being an Olympian. I wanted to be chosen by the Gods because I thought I'd be able to see my mom again."

Sidney Mills did not live to see his son's Olympic dream come true. He suffered a fatal stroke, and at age twelve Billy was an orphan.

Yet Billy's dream lived on – even when others tried to dash it.

As a high school freshman, Billy was kept off the track team because he was considered too small. The last meet of the season, he convinced the coach to let him run in the half-mile and mile races. As an unofficial team member without a uniform, the too-small freshman lined up at the back of pack . . .

. . . "And I won both races," Mills remembers, and proudly still.

Small boy, big heart – like Little Colin of the AYSO Golden Eagles. As a sophomore, Billy won the state high school cross-country championship. He went undefeated his junior and senior years.

His exploits led him to the University of Kansas in

1958 and eventually to Tokyo for the 1964 Olympics where, on a warm summer night, Billy Mills ran a 10,000-meter race for the Gods.

With less than one lap remaining, Billy was in position to shock the Olympic world. He was running abreast world-record holder Ron Clarke of Australia with Mohamad Gammoundi of Tunisia right on their heels.

Then push came to nudge.

"Clarke was boxed in and he pushed me a couple of times," Mills recounted. "I nudged him back to hold my ground. Then he put his arm under my arm and pushed me into the next lane.

"Gammoudi saw this as his opportunity to strike," Mills continued. "He pushed me one way and Clarke the other. I thought I was going to fall down."

Mills somehow managed to stay on his feet, but the damage was done. He lost his stride and fell behind by ten meters with only one-hundred-and-fifty meters to go.

"I've got to go now," Mills recalls thinking as he regained his rhythm. Just then a German runner who had already been lapped moved over, allowing Billy room to pass on the inside coming off the final curve. Perhaps more important than the gesture of sportsmanship was the eagle emblem on the German's singlet.

"I saw that beautiful eagle and it was so inspiring," Mills shared, and then explained why. "When my mom died, my dad stroked my arm and told me, 'I know you have broken wings. I'll share a secret with you – someday you'll have the wings to fly like an eagle.' "

In Native American culture, God sends messages through animals: Mills, who is seven-sixteenths Lakota, saw that embroidered eagle as encouragement from his father.

"I started lifting my knees and pumping my arms and reaching with my feet," Mills said. Suddenly running as if with eagle wings on his feet, Mills caught Clarke and Gammoudi thirty meters from glory, passed them both, and crossed the finish line in an Olympic-record time of 28 minutes, 24.4 seconds.

On the victory stand, America's first – and still only – 10,000-meter Olympic Gold Medalist cried. "I felt the force of my dad," Billy Mills confided. "I felt his touch, not on my skin but *under* my skin."

Stroking his arm, the broken eagle wing?

"Yes," he answered emotionally, repeating emphatically: "Yes."

Billy Mills' dream had come true. His broken wings were finally mended. By any measure, society's or Coach Wooden's, he was a true success.

Fifteen

The Free Throw

"Although it is all right to want to win, remember that you are a winner when you know you made the effort to do the best of which you are capable of regardless of what others may think."

— John Wooden,

in a letter to Dallas and Greg

Δ

The following essay that Dallas wrote when she was in the eighth grade about a true personal experience reveals just how close to heart she had already taken Coach Wooden's lessons on doing one's best to earn peace of mind and true success.

Δ

"Dallas! Time to come in for dinner!" my mom called.

"Okay, give me a sec – just one more shot!" I took a deep breath, gazing up at the basketball hoop in our driveway. I shuffled my feet to the perfect position: right foot one inch behind the free-throw line, left foot a couple more inches back. I dribbled once, twice. Took another breath. Feeling the basketball's firm, familiar weight in my hands, I lifted it up to shooting position, bent my knees, and released.

The ball soared towards the hoop in a straight, graceful arc, swishing cleanly through the net. Score! Twenty-four out of twenty-five free throws in a row. Almost perfect, but not quite. To me, it wasn't good enough.

After dinner, I went back outside and shot free throw after free throw until the sun set and it became too dark to make out the hoop against the night sky.

The next morning, my mom drove me to the big free-throw shooting contest for which I had spent countless hours practicing. Nerves clenching my stomach, I was quiet during the two-hour drive to the regional finals. If I won this contest, I would move on to the California state finals competition.

It was the time of year when my mom was busiest at work. She was manager of her division and I knew she could use her weekend to rest. But here she was, taking an entire Saturday to cheerfully drive down with me and root me on as my dad, a sports columnist, was away covering a Los Angeles Lakers game. More than anything, I wanted to make them and my little brother Greggie proud.

We arrived at the high school gym where the competition was being held. The drumbeat of bouncing basketballs echoed off the walls as kids warmed up before the big event. The stands were crowded with people. I pictured myself out there alone on the basketball court, shooting free throws in front of everyone, and my nervousness compounded.

"Don't be nervous, Sweetheart!" my mom said, as if sensing my anxiety. "You'll do great! You've been practicing for months!" She helped me check in at the registration table, and then it was time for me to venture onto the basketball court to start warming up. Mom gave me a good-luck hug and headed for the stands.

There were a handful of other girls competing in my age division. The competition was structured so that we each shot five free throws in a row per round, with five rounds for a total of twenty-five free throws. The girl with the highest score at the end would move on to the statewide championships.

When my first turn came, I walked out to the free-throw line searching for my mom's face in the crowd. She caught my eye and gave a little wave, smiling at me. It reminded me of when I met legendary coach John Wooden and he told me he always caught his wife's eye in the stands before his basketball games. I felt my nerves lessen and reminded myself of all the free throws I had practiced shooting in my driveway at home. Again, Coach Wooden's words gave me added confidence because he says, "Failing to prepare is preparing to fail." I knew I had prepared to do my best!

Swish, swish, swish, swish, swish. I made all five free throws my first turn.

My confidence increased as the competition went on. Soon there were only two of us in the lead, neck and neck. We both went ten-for-ten, then fifteen-for-fifteen, then twenty-for-twenty. It was turning into a real shootout!

The other girl took her final turn. *Swish, swish, swish, swish, swish.* A perfect twenty-five for twenty-five. I would have to make all five of my final free throws to force us into a tiebreaker. I had done this before in my driveway; in fact, my record was thirty-one straight!

I took a deep breath as I strode to the line. My mom gave me a thumbs-up from the stands.

Swish. Swish. Swish. Swish.

One more shot. I just needed to make this final free throw to stay in the competition and force overtime.

I shuffled my feet to the perfect position: shoulder-width apart with the right foot one inch behind the free-throw line, left foot a couple more inches back. I followed my routine: I dribbled once, twice. Took a deep breath and focused on the front of the rim. I lifted the basketball up to shooting position, bent my knees, and released.

The aim was straight and true and the arch was perfect . . . but the ball came up a little short . . . and hit the front of the rim . . . bounced softly once . . . and then spun around the rim as if in slow motion. Suddenly the gym was hold-your-breath-quiet as everyone watched the basketball roll around the hoop . . . rolling, rolling, rolling . . .

. . . *out.*

I had missed one shot. Like my final shot, I had come up short. My final score was an excellent twenty-four out of twenty-five – but I had needed a perfect twenty-five out of twenty-five to stay alive.

After all that hard work, after all those hours and weeks and months of practice, after the long drive on a Saturday morning, I had lost the competition. For a moment, I felt like a failure as I fought back my tears and congratulated the ecstatic winner.

I shuffled towards the stands, towards my waiting mother. I looked down at my feet. Around me, the bouncing of many basketballs seemed to echo sadly on the gym floor. Mom greeted me with a huge smile as she enveloped me in a tight hug. "Dallas, you were fantastic out there!" she said.

"But I lost," I sniffled. "I missed that last free throw."

"That's okay," my mom said, gently lifting up my face to meet her eyes. "Some things are out of our control.

Sometimes the ball just doesn't roll in." She reminded me of Coach Wooden's definition of success being "peace of mind which is a direct result of self-satisfaction in knowing you did your best to become the best you are capable of becoming."

"Did you try your best?" Mom asked.

"Of course," I said.

"Did you put in the effort and practice as much as you could?"

"Yes."

"Then you're a true success," my mom concluded. "Coach Wooden would be proud of you. I could not be any prouder of you. Dad and Greggie will be super proud, too. Why don't you call Dad right now and tell him how great you did."

I never thought that losing a free-throw contest would boost my self-esteem, but it did. I was able to find pride and confidence in myself, no matter the circumstance. I was able to separate "success" from "winning" and "perfection."

I often think back to Coach Wooden's definition of success, especially when "the ball doesn't bounce my way" in life, and I keep striving to be the best person I am capable of being.

Sixteen

Yosemite Falls

———

"Players with fight never lose, they just run out of time."
– John Wooden

Δ

Coach always enjoyed hearing what Dallas and Greg were up to, about the heights they literally rose to as chronicled in the three following chapters. Each story brought a smile to Coach's face because the feats were testament to the character traits in the Pyramid of Success.

Δ

"Now I know how Sisyphus felt," the companion, sweaty and thirsty and weary – not from pushing one stone up a mountainside, but from an hour of climbing an endless uphill rocky path of switchbacks – said to the Mountain Boy.

"Hey, we're not sissies!" the seven-year-old

Mountain Boy replied, having never before heard the tale of the Greek king sentenced to rolling a rock up a mountain in Hades again and again, endlessly, for eternity.

The Mountain Boy was not content to just climb to the mountain's summit. He aimed to get there fast, in record time, ahead of everyone already in front of him. It was as though a birthday party was taking place at the peak and he was late for it.

"Come on, let's pass 'em," the Mountain Boy urged every time a climber or group was spotted ahead.

It was the Mountain Boy's very first true hike, and he had chosen a doozy. The rugged trail led to the top of Yosemite Falls, the fifth-highest waterfall on the planet – and the highest in North America – with a total drop of 2,245 feet.

The trail from base to summit measures 3.8 miles. The final 3.5 miles are vertically *straight up*. If anyone claims otherwise, it is a lie.

"It's going to be an eight-mile roundtrip," the companion warned earlier, hoping to steer the first-grader Mountain Boy to a shorter, easier hike. But the Mountain Boy dearly loves waterfalls, almost as dearly as he loves soft serve vanilla ice cream and his boxer dog Garfield – Gar for short, who also loves vanilla ice cream. And so to the trailhead of Yosemite Falls the father and son headed at high noon under a baking July sun.

Without first eating lunch. Or even packing one. Indeed, their only provisions were a liter of bottled water and an eight-ounce Wild Cherry Squeezit fruit drink, the Mountain Boy's beverage of choice. The only way they could have been less prepared would have been to leave their socks and shoes back in the car.

Spartan rations, however, seemed more than sufficient because the companion wholly figured the Mountain Boy would want to turn back after fifteen or twenty minutes. He underestimated the Mountain Boy, and greatly. The Mountain Boy proved to be stubborn as a mule, not to mention as sure-footed a climber.

And so, on and on, up and up, the two climbed. Higher and higher, all the while passing each and every hiker who dared to dawdle. Steadily the switchbacks grew rockier and steeper and more precarious. Steadily their ascent continued. The trail became as tough as Fort Knox's front door. The Mountain Boy was undaunted.

"Every day is a winding road," he jokingly sang over and over, that being the only lyric the Mountain Boy seemed to know from Sheryl Crow's hit pop song of that summer.

After an hour on the winding stone stairway towards heaven, the two reached a precipice overlooking the beautiful Yosemite Valley far below while affording an eagle's-eye view of the waterfall still looming high above.

"Not bad for two dudes 'fraid of heights, huh?" the Mountain Boy said, and proudly, as he stood seemingly on the rim of the world.

It was breathtaking. It was worth the tiring climb. It was worth the heel blisters. And it was time to head back down.

"No, we've got to go all the way to the tippity-top," the Mountain Boy insisted.

"You're almost there," a friendly stranger making his descent offered encouragingly. "Just another fifteen minutes."

Fifteen minutes – only if you happen to be a Desert Bighorn sheep.

Thirty minutes of continuous climbing later the summit was still fifteen minutes away by the estimate of another descending hiker.

By now the Mountain Boy had finished off the water bottle and the companion worried about him suffering dehydration. He again suggested they turn around and head back down.

"We've come this far," the Mountain Boy contested and, apparently remembering the earlier mention of Sisyphus, added: "We're not sissy kings. Let's keep going to the top. We can do it."

After some debate and pleading, it was agreed if

they did not reach the summit in fifteen more minutes, they would turn back.

Twenty minutes later, exactly two hours and fifteen minutes after they had begun their uphill journey, the end of the rainbow was now in sight. Now it was for sure no more than ten minutes further.

Ten minutes, but in the growing heat and with no water left. The companion made the tough call: "Let's head back down," he said, knowing they had the two-plus hours of ascent *behind* them still ahead of them on descent.

"But we're not quitters. Come on, let's keep going," the Mountain Boy protested, though less resolutely than before.

In many ways it would have been easier to finish the ascent. Ten minutes, and surely another climber would share some water and even a sandwich or energy bar with the Mountain Boy. But the companion thought another lesson could be learned here: That sometimes the thrill of victory pales to the thrill of trying.

"The better part of valor is discretion," the companion explained, quoting one of the few lines of Shakespeare he knows by heart. When the words soared over the Mountain Boys' head like an elegant hawk in the Yosemite sky above, the companion quoted the great philosopher John Wooden: "Success is never final. Failure is never fatal. It's courage that counts." Perhaps no greater lesson could be learned. By both the Mountain Boy and then man.

Already the Mountain Boy had gone nearly two hours higher than expected. He had every reason to be proud of himself. He had indeed displayed courage.

The Mountain Boy listened thoughtfully and replied, "OK, as long as we're not quitters or sissies like that Greek king you told me about."

And with that the companion pulled out the Wild Cherry Squeezit. After slugging down half of the delicious sweet nectar, the Mountain Boy stopped, wiped his lips with the back of his hand, and offered his companion the rest.

The companion thanked him, but told the Mountain Boy to go ahead and finish it.

No. The Mountain Boy insisted on sharing. "I think you need it," he observed.

As the companion took a few tasty sips, it struck him that it is indeed true there comes a time when a boy becomes father to the man – and that perhaps this was a glimpse into a crystal ball of that future day. In thirty years, or perhaps forty, would these two come back here, this time with the Mountain Boy's hand doing the holding and the steadying and the helping as the son and father rise up the mountain? As Hemingway's closing words in *The Sun Also Rises* beautifully put it: "Isn't it pretty to think so?"

The footing on the descent of the Yosemite Falls trail is arguably more treacherous than on the climb. And so, as they had going up, the Mountain Boy and his companion held sweaty hands the entire way down. For four-and-a-half hours they were linked this way, as though crossing a busy street. Bonding-wise it definitely beat sitting in the bleachers at a ballgame. It is a frozen moment of memory the companion will hold hands with for the rest of his life journey.

By adventure's end, the Mountain Boy came into focus like a Mountain *Man*. Not once during the marathon march did he complain. Not one single, "Why didn't you bring more water?" No whining of "I'm hungry" or "I'm tired." No pout, always a smile.

Afterward, the Mountain Boy was greeted like a hero by the rest of his family as well as by fellow climbers he had seen on the mountain. And deservedly so. No matter that he came up ten minutes short of the summit: he was a hero for what he did accomplish, not judged for what he did not.

At dinner in a restaurant that evening, the Mountain Boy spotted a photograph of Yosemite Falls. It was the famous black-and-white image taken by Ansel Adams. Ironically, the Mountain Boy's middle name is Ansel, albeit in honor of his great grandpa. The Mountain Boy still thought this coincidence was cool.

Laws forbid taking anything out of a National Park. Yet the Mountain Boy and his companion had certainly brought something down off the mountain. Instead of stones in their pockets, they each took away a piece of Yosemite Falls in their hearts. Too, they left with Ansel Adams' awe-inspiring photo etched in their minds.

"This was the best day of my life," the Mountain Boy said when he was getting tucked into bed that night, smiling as purely as the day he picked out Gar from a litter of five and brought him home as a puppy.

Of course there is no "best" day, no day that is the ultimate masterpiece above all others, only different shades in the rainbow. This day had been a beautiful hue of orange, the Mountain Boy's favorite color, or maybe sky blue.

No, that's not quite right. It was a red-letter day. Wild-cherry red, like a Squeezit.

Seventeen

The Rematch

────

*"If you stay intent and your ability warrants it, you will
eventually reach the top of the mountain."*

– John Wooden

Δ

On a hallway just outside the eight-year-old Mountain
Boy's bedroom, where he sees it a dozen or more times
each day, hangs a framed photograph of Yosemite Falls. It is
a black-and-white print of one of Ansel Adams' most
famous photos.

It is the Mountain Boy's favorite photo. Even over
his Steve Prefontaine running poster and autographed race
photo of Olympic gold medalist Billy Mills.

And yet for the previous year, for a dozen or more
times a day, the dear photograph has haunted the
Mountain Boy. It has reminded him, not of failure exactly,
but of unfinished business certainly.

While the Mountain Boy had the time of his young

life during the climb – even painting pictures of Yosemite Falls every time his second-grade class did art – he was also greatly disappointed about not reaching the "tippity-top." He eagerly insisted on a rematch.

And so, before the blister on his right heel fully healed, reservations were made for July 12 the following summer. The Mountain Boy circled the date on his calendar, a holiday as dearly anticipated as his eighth birthday and Christmas.

Exactly one year and one day after his first attempt, the Mountain Boy got his wish: a rematch with the tallest waterfall in North America at 2,425 feet.

This time the Mountain Boy and his companion were not guilty of the Wooden-ism, "Failing to prepare is preparing to fail." They came loaded with previsions for the excursion and the eighty-degree summer temperature, bringing along enough water and Gatorade to get a camel across the Sahara as well as fruit roll-ups, home-baked chocolate-chip cookies and, for a victory lunch at the summit, four slices of cold pepperoni pizza leftover from their pre-climb carbo-loading dinner the previous evening.

As you can probably tell, the Mountain Boy did the packing. And his companion did the carrying. However, the companion did exact a promise that in twenty years he gets to do the packing and the Mountain Boy will be the working Sherpa.

The 3.8-mile climb from base to summit includes about sixty steep and rocky switchbacks. Instead of repeating the Sheryl Crow lyric, *"Every day is a winding road,"* this time the Mountain Boy occasionally interrupted his engaging non-stop chatter to sing from a different pop song. From Savage Garden's "Truly, Madly, Deeply." From the heart. *"I want to stand with you on a mountain."*

After two hours and fifty-five minutes, after five dozen switchbacks, after passing the spot where he had grown light-headed and dizzy and been forced to turn back three-hundred-and-sixty-six days prior, the Mountain Boy truly and happily stood with his companion on the top of a mountain.

On the top of the world. On the "tippity-top" of Yosemite Falls. The Mountain Boy gave his companion a heartfelt 2,425-foot-high-five.

"We made it!" the Mountain Boy cheered, beaming like he had just won an Olympic gold medal.

"I never doubted you would," the companion replied, even more breathless from the view than from the climb to see it. "This is beautiful."

"No, it's better than that," observed the Mountain Boy, showing wisdom well beyond his eight-and-a-half years. "It's perfect."

Perfect. Two slices of pizza each and some chocolate-chip cookies made it even more so. All washed down by two Wild Cherry Squeezits that had been selected for this happy occasion as carefully as a vintage bottle of champagne. The Mountain Boy even provided a toast: "I thought last year was the best day of my life, but today is a hundred times better. I never dreamed it would be this great."

No, better than that. Perfect.

Perfect because there is nothing more admirable in sports – in life, really – than setting a goal, coming up short, and then trying again until you succeed. "Fall down seven times, get up eight," states an ancient proverb. Is there any lesson more worthwhile? Any accomplishment more fulfilling than one earned over the long haul?

The affirmative answer was readily evident on that mountain. I saw it on the Mountain Boy's tanned-and-determined face during the ascent and later in his proud shining eyes at the summit.

I see it still, a decade and a half later. See it each time the Mountain Boy – now a six-foot-three-inch young man – walks past the framed Ansel Adams photograph hanging beside a blue-and-gold Pyramid of Success that represents a mountain itself; pauses while his green eyes navigate a black-and-white path to the "tippity-top" of Yosemite Falls; and smiles nobly as he reflects on his victorious rematch.

I smile, too. Coach Wooden knowingly used Patience and Faith as mortar in the Pyramid. The Mountain Boy and his companion had started at the base with Industriousness and Enthusiasm – and they reached Competitive Greatness and Success at the apex. Together.

Eighteen

Rising To A Tall Challenge

"Some of my greatest pleasures have come from finding ways to overcome obstacles."

– John Wooden

Δ

The culminating peak of the Sierra Nevada mountain range was discovered by a California State Geological Survey team in 1864 and named Mount Whitney in honor of the team's leader, Josiah Dwight Whitney.

During that trip, survey team member Clarence King attempted to ascend its summit.

Twice.

Both times he failed.

It was not until his third attempt nearly a decade later on September 19, 1873 that King successfully reached the peak of the tallest mountain in the contiguous United States. Ironically, today one in three climbers statistically makes it to the summit of Mount Whitney.

King's feat, however, did not make history. His was actually the fourth successful climb. The historic first ascent was made a month earlier by three local fishermen friends – Charley Begole, Johnny Lucas and Al Johnson – who reached the 14,496-foot summit at noon on August 19, 1873.

A century of summers later – on July 26, 2003 and also at high noon – came another successful ascent of the mountain briefly known as "Fisherman's Peak" but which soon reverted back to its original name of Mount Whitney.

Unlike Begole, Lucas, and Johnson, my then sixteen-year-old daughter Dallas Nicole and my wife Lisa took a cell phone to the summit and called home: "Hi Dad! We made it! It's *soooo* beautiful up here! I feel like I'm on the top of the world!"

Sir Edmund Hillary was the first person to actually stand on the top of the world, reaching Mount Everest's peak on May 29, 1953. Dallas was born thirty-four years later on May 29. The coincidence of date had piqued her interest on the golden anniversary of Hillary's historic climb in 2003. She set the goal of standing, if not on the top of the world, on the top of the lower forty-eight states.

Keeping in mind Coach Wooden's admonishment that "proper preparation and self-discipline can dispel fear and doubt," daughter and mother practiced for their quest with Saturday morning hikes that began at a few miles and eventually stretched to ten miles. Impressive, but still less than half the twenty-two-mile round trip of a successful Mount Whitney journey.

"I have some doubts I'll be able to make it to the top," Lisa, who during the previous twenty years of our marriage (and eleven more since) I cannot recall failing at anything, confided before they left for their climb.

"I *know* I'll do it," Dallas, who at the time ran track and cross-country in high school, told me separately and confidently.

Their journey began at Mt. Whitney's trail portal at four in the morning. Guided by miners' head-mounted flashlights as well as bright moonlight, and also by their glowing excitement, daughter led mother across one stream by carefully stepping on slippery rocks and another by walking on logs.

The sunrise, they marveled later, was worthy of a painting or at least belonged on postcard. So, too, were the lakes and waterfalls and wildflowers they saw along their ascent.

Each shouldering a daypack filled with enough water and Gatorade to run a marathon, they rose above the tree line after five miles.

A mile later they reached the switchbacks. The infamous switchbacks that echo those of Yosemite Falls climbed by the Mountain Boy and his companion a few years earlier. There are, by actual count, ninety-seven switchbacks covering 2.2 steep and jagged miles leading from Trail Camp (with an elevation of 12,000 feet) to Trail Crest (with an elevation of 13,777 feet).

The ankle-twisting switchbacks are daunting, but the most difficult leg of the climb follows. Even a mountain sheep would have trouble with the footing on the final two miles to the summit. Add in air so rarefied it makes lungs gasp and heads ache, and each step becomes a true challenge.

The daughter and mother felt snow and felt fear, felt fatigue and felt like turning back, and at high noon they felt the elation of a difficult challenge conquered. Eight hours and a half-dozen blisters after they set forth in cold darkness, the pair enjoyed the same lofty view three fishermen friends had first witnessed one-hundred-and-thirty summers earlier.

"It's breathtaking," Dallas, intending no pun, said on the cell phone.

It was breathtaking for me to hear her words, for as mentioned previously Dallas had needed breathing tubes when she was born three months prematurely. "She's a real fighter," the doctor said back then, Dallas' fragile life balancing on a dangerous precipice, and he was so very right. As a competitive youth track and cross-country runner, Dallas drew strength from her past and in fact made "P.A.S.T." – Preemies Are So Tough – her personal mantra.

"When I felt like I was about to die in a race, I reminded myself how blessed I was to be alive," Dallas recalls. "If I could survive being born weighing a sickly two pounds, six ounces, I knew I could survive the rest of any race. While I wasn't an elite runner, I made varsity and with this attitude I always passed some runners in the late stages of races."

She needed this steely strength and powerful mantra during her sophomore year in high school when she faced a new physical challenge: "compartment syndrome" in both shins. Surgery only partially relieved the pain. No matter. Dallas courageously returned to competition her junior and senior seasons. She was even voted Most Inspirational by her cross-country teammates as she further epitomized Coach Wooden's maxim: "Some of my greatest pleasures have come from finding ways to overcome obstacles."

Born a fighter, Dallas says being an athlete further fortified her fortitude: "If I wasn't a runner, I wouldn't have made it to the top of Mt. Whitney." Making it to the peak was no small feat for Dallas or Lisa, which is why it was such a big deal for them both. As Coach Wooden noted: "We get stronger when we test ourselves. Adversity can make us better. We must be challenged to improve, and adversity is the challenger."

The two newly crowned champions of the tall challenge snapped a dozen celebratory pictures and proudly signed the registry book at the Summit Hut. Then, chased by threatening clouds and thunderclaps, after just twenty minutes of rest they began their six-hour, eleven-mile descent.

The daughter brought down from Mount Whitney's summit a tiny granite stone, a keepsake reminder that this former preemie is indeed so tough of mind and body.

Her mother and climbing companion brought down something less concrete, but no less important: a strengthened belief in herself.

Even today, even at sea level, Dallas and Lisa still feel on top of the world.

Nineteen

Help Others

———

*"What you are as a person is far more important than
what you are as a basketball player."*

— John Wooden

Δ

Coach Wooden put into daily practice his belief that "you can't live a perfect day without doing something for someone who will never be able to repay you." Two small examples: he graciously signed autographs even when the request interrupted his meal, and he paid for the stamps himself to mail back items sent to him to be autographed that did not include return postage.

His deeds and words have greatly inspired both my children ever since they were quite young.

"What you really are is more important than what others perceive you to be," Coach wrote in a letter addressed jointly to Dallas and Greg. "Character is more important than reputation."

Dallas memorably showed her character and desire to help others in the fifth grade when she applied for and received a fifty-dollar grant from the school district to fund a creative project. She put together a collection of her own original short stories and poems, drew some black-and-white illustrations, and took the forty-page manuscript to a local copy shop where she used all of the grant money to print twenty-five staple-bound books.

Dallas's idea was to sell the volumes at her elementary school and then use the proceeds to repay the grant she had received so that an extra one could be offered the following year.

To Dallas' great surprise, she sold every single copy of *There's a Huge Pimple On My Nose* within two days. Moreover, students and teachers and parents excitedly asked when more copies would be available. So Dallas went back to Kinko's and ordered twenty-five more copies of *Pimple* which again sold out quickly. After doing so a third time – and after *The Los Angeles Times* wrote a glowing review that concluded, "If you simply want to enjoy some remarkable writing, it would be hard to find a book more satisfying" – Dallas went to a professional print shop and ordered a large batch of glue-bound, glossy-covered copies.

Dallas ended up funding not one but *two* additional grants in her name the following year. *Pimple* remains popular with young readers and to date has sold more than three thousand copies all across the United States, fairly amazing considering its modest beginning.

Seven years after *Pimple* during her senior year in high school, Dallas wrote and self-published her second book – *3 a.m.* – which is also a collection of short stories that received high literary praise. In fact, she was invited to appear on the Emmy-winning national PBS book talk show "Between The Lines" hosted by the extremely talented and charismatic Barry Kibrick. At age eighteen, Dallas was – and remains – the youngest guest to have ever appeared on the show.

Serendipitously, Dallas taped her appearance at the KLCS-TV studio in downtown Los Angeles on the very same gorgeous spring afternoon in 2006 as the show's oldest guest – John Wooden, then ninety-five. Coach was being interviewed about his newest book, co-written with Steve Jamison, *Wooden On Leadership: How to Create a Winning Organization.*

You can imagine our delighted surprise upon walking into the "green room" and seeing Coach there. The currents of my life had once more fortuitously brought us together. Kibrick experienced equal marvel when, before he could politely make proper introductions, Coach greeted us by name and simultaneously gave Dallas and Greg a warm hug hello. Picking up right from when he had shown my Little Ones the talking toy ape in the red vest years earlier,

Coach became the Self-Esteem Wizard once more by asking Dallas if she would sign a copy of *3 a.m.* for him in exchange for an autographed copy of his new book. Such rare grace was so routinely typical for Coach.

Dallas was, understandably, extremely nervous before her on-camera interview. But she says seeing Coach put her at ease. She also thought of his maxim – "Success is never final. Failure is never fatal. It's courage that counts" – and focused on being courageous rather than worrying about "winning." As a result, instead of being a nerve-wracking experience, Dallas recalls feeling relaxed and enjoying discussing her book with Barry Kibrick.

Dallas used proceeds from the sales of *3 a.m.* to further her commitment to helping others by funding "Write On! For Literacy" (writeonbooks.org), the nonprofit foundation she created as an eighth-grader in 2001 to encourage kids to read and write. That December she also held a Write On! Holiday Book Drive that collected and donated more than two-hundred new books to disadvantaged kids its first year; the annual effort has now given away more than twelve-thousand books. She has also spoken at well over one hundred elementary, middle, and high schools.

At the beginning of her talks Dallas always asks her young audience if anyone wants to be a writer: typically only one or two hands go up, sometimes none. At the end

•

of her presentation she asks the same question and invariably this time numerous arms shoot up excitedly. The reason, Dallas has found, is that too often students simply don't think young people can be writers. She lets them know otherwise.

Dallas extended her advocacy for young writers by creating her own publishing company in 2011. It's first book, *Dancing With The Pen*, is a two-hundred-and-eighty-page anthology of short stories and poems written exclusively *by* young writers *for* young readers. In fact, it features more than sixty youth in elementary school, middle school and high school from all across the United States as well as from Canada, Singapore, and New Zealand.

Each stride along her Write On! journey – as well as time happily spent assisting senior citizens with household chores; volunteering at local food pantries; and her inspiring 2013 "Year of Kindness Challenge" with a weekly entry posted on her blog, fittingly titled daybydaymasterpiece.com – Dallas has found truth in Coach Wooden's words: "There is great joy in doing something for somebody else with no thought of receiving anything in return."

Greg has followed in his big sister's philanthropic footsteps. He suffered a hip stress fracture that sidelined him from cross-country and track as a high school freshman. Then knee troubles ruined his sophomore seasons as well. For a boy who has loved to run and race since he was seven years old, including competing in a number of youth national cross country championship meets, the back-to-back setbacks were crushing. In Greg's words: "Running is hard, but *not* running is harder."

However, rather than feel sorry for himself and focusing on what he could not do, Greg decided to find joy in doing something for others. He emphasized with kids who could not enjoy the benefits of running – such as boosted self-esteem and confidence, new friendships, and improved physical fitness – not because they were injured, but because they could not afford running shoes.

In October 2006, Greg set a goal of collecting one hundred pairs of running shoes in good condition to donate to disadvantaged youth by the upcoming Christmas. He tirelessly spread word of his cause and collected – and personally scrubbed by hand – more than *five hundred* pairs of running shoes that he then sent to an orphanage and youth sports program in Uganda. He was hooked. His short three-month project became a longtime commitment even after he regained his running health.

At age sixteen Greg created his own nonprofit organization "Give Running" (giverunning.org) and since 2006 he has collected more than 14,000 pairs of running and athletic shoes, thousands of which he has personally washed by hand. These shoes have been sent to youth living in impoverished villages in numerous developing countries as well as to inner-city communities across the United States. Greg has even visited West Africa twice – Mali for ten days in December 2009 and Ghana for seventeen days in December 2011 – on humanitarian trips for Give Running.

After graduating from the University of Southern California in May 2012 he delayed his plan to purse an MBA in Social Entrepreneurship for one year in order to focus his energies on expanding Give Running's reach and positive impact; this included a month-long humanitarian trip to Sri Lanka in 2013. Greg is now a member of the USC Marshall School of Business MBA Class of 2015 and aims to work with social-good enterprises after he graduates.

In addition to being deeply inspired to help others by Coach Wooden, Dallas and Greg have been blessed to have Mike and Bob Bryan – the winningest doubles tandem in tennis history – as key role models in their lives. Coach Wooden was a fan of Mike and Bob, for their sportsmanship as well as their athletic skills, he told me when I asked him to sign a Pyramid of Success as a gift for them.

Because the identical twins remember the childhood thrills they felt when getting autographs from their tennis heroes, Mike and Bob try to return the favor to today's young fans. It is not unusual for them to spend half an hour or more after a match or a practice session signing autographs courtside.

"We feel it's important to make time for fans," says Mike.

Adds Bob: "It only takes a moment to make a kid smile, so why not take the time and make the effort to maybe make a small difference?"

How Wooden-like does that sound?

Mike and Bob's time and effort often make more than a small difference. Through their nonprofit organization The Bryan Bros. Foundation they have supplied rackets to inner-city high school tennis teams; supported youth tennis leagues; sponsored young players with equipment and travel expenses; and in countless other ways succeeded in their mission to "help at-risk survive and thrive."

But perhaps never have Mike and Bob stood taller than when they made time for Shigeki Sumitani, a ten-year-old from Japan. When he emailed the Bryan Brothers asking for an autograph, they happily obliged.

A few weeks later, upon first learning that Shigeki was battling cancer, Mike and Bob solemnly signed a tennis ball and cap and also mailed the small boy one of the shirts they wore while winning their first Grand Slam championship at the French Open.

When they next learned that Shigeki's father had bought autographed, match-used rackets of his son's two other favorite players – Andy Roddick and Andre Agassi – on eBay, only to receive two unsigned knockoff rackets, Mike and Bob autographed one of the rackets they had just used in the French Open final and sent it by FedEx to him.

A small thing? Perhaps. But not to Shigeki. To him it made far more than a small difference. To him it meant the world. As Coach Wooden observed: "Sometimes the smallest gestures make the biggest difference."

Shigeki passed away only a few days after that priority package arrived. He was wearing the championship shirt from the French Open, with the racket from that same match at his side, while listening to the "Five-Setter" music CD the Bryan Brothers Band had recently produced.

These kind gestures provided a little happiness when happiness had long before been chased away. Shigeki's mother died at age thirty of a heart attack when her son was six years old, soon followed by his cancer diagnosis that very year. The cancer grew worse and worse. So did the pain.

"At the end, he knew his time was short," said the elder Sumitani. "His treatments were very hard on him. Frequently he had attacks of severe pain. Sometimes he couldn't sleep. Sometimes he made complaints. But he did his best."

So did the Bryans. They sent Shigeki autographs and shoes and CDs and emails. Most importantly, they sent him the knowledge that they cared. Indeed, Bob and Mike embodied the Wooden-like words that their mother Kathy, a former professional tennis star herself, has preached to them since childhood: "It's far more important who you are as person than who you are as an athlete."

An only child, Shigeki used to tell his father he dearly wished he had a brother. Briefly, he got the next best thing: two long-distance surrogate big brothers. "Having the Bryans as his 'older brothers' made him happy," the boy's father confided to me.

Under much happier conditions, Mike and Bob have similarly been surrogate big brothers to Dallas and Greg, showing them endless support over the years. Many times when Greg needed it most – when stress fractures derailed his running on three different occasions or when he was a Rhodes Scholar Finalist but learned the ultimate opportunity to study abroad had eluded him – Mike and Bob have sent emails of encouragement. They have done the same during Dallas's own tough times.

Conversely, in recognition of Dallas' high points – her successful ascent of Mount Whitney; acceptance into college and graduate school; receiving the 2013-14 John

Steinbeck Fellowship – Mike and Bob sent congratulatory flowers and text messages. Greg, too, has experienced the thrill of their kind gestures.

Dallas and Greg have emulated their big-brother role models by making small gestures to Mike and Bob in return. When the twins are home during a rare break from the pro tour, Dallas likes to bake "Friendship Bread" for them. And Greg has helped do their laundry. Wayne Bryan still happily recalls the time when this was not such a small thing after his twin sons had returned from a three-month clay-court season in Europe: "Greg and I did a world-record thirteen loads of wash, drying, and folding at the local Camarillo Coin Op Laundry. It took us some two and a half hours. We really chopped some wood. He had a smile on his face the whole time and we shared some laughs and he did a beautiful job and it was a day I'll never forget."

Greg feels the same way. There truly is great joy – and great memories created – in helping others.

Δ

My tradition of putting quotes by Coach Wooden in Dallas' and Greg's sack lunches extended from grade school all the way though high school graduation. It continued even when they went away to college and grad school and continues still – only instead of in their lunch boxes I now send them a daily Wooden-ism by text message or email. Almost as often, they send them to me too.

The positive impact of Coach's words and life lessons on Dallas and Greg are far reaching. Consider one of my favorite Wooden-isms that I have repeated numerous times in these pages already: "Things turn out best for those who make the best of the way things turn out."

Dallas kept this in mind when she decided to stop playing high school basketball after two seasons, in great part because of her painful compartment syndrome. She also took to heart Coach Wooden's advice: "Don't let what you cannot do interfere with what you can do." What she could do was redirect her energy and talents; she took advantage of the new free slot in her school schedule to take a drama class. Moreover, without daily basketball practices she used her newfound time to write a full-length play titled "The 74-Year-Old Rookie" about an elderly gentleman and his relationship with a group of baseball-playing neighborhood kids.

Then she pitched it to the drama department director. This was a bold proposal because her high school had never before produced a student-written play. However, as Mark Twain once wisely wrote: "Twenty years from now you will be more disappointed by the things that you didn't do than by the ones you did do. So throw off the bowlines. Sail away from the safe harbor. Catch the trade winds in your sails. Explore. Dream. Discover." Or, in words from Coach Wooden that Dallas was more familiar with: "The man who is afraid to risk failure seldom has to face success."

Dallas took the risk, threw off her bowlines, and achieved her new dream: "The 74-Year-Old Rookie" was a grand success. Dallas wrote another school play the following year as a senior and, flash forward, has now won numerous awards as a playwright. Her play "A Frog In Boiling Water" was even performed in the prestigious 2012 Samuel French Off-Off Broadway Short Play Festival in New York City. That is indeed making things turn out for the best.

Similarly, Greg overcame the adversity posed by collegiate injuries to be named the Distance Captain on the USC Men's Track & Field Team as a senior four-year walk-on. But what would have pleased Coach Wooden even more was that Greg was also named to the Pacific-12 Conference All-Academic First Team; was given the Willis O. Hunter Award for being USC's student-athlete with the highest graduating GPA (3.966); was the 2012 male recipient of the revered Pac-12 Conference Leadership Award; and was a 2012 Rhodes Scholar Finalist.

Academics were also paramount for Dallas, who, like her younger brother, attended the University of Southern California on a full merit Trustee Scholarship and graduated *summa cum laude*. She then went to Purdue University – Coach Wooden's alma mater! – where she earned her Master of Fine Arts degree in Fiction Writing. She also taught English each semester during her postgraduate studies at Purdue, something that again would have pleased Coach immensely.

Dallas, who plans to continue combining university teaching with authoring novels and plays, shared the story of her childhood visit with Coach Wooden to her students on the final day of each class she taught at Purdue. Her words included these:

"Meeting Coach Wooden was a life-changing experience that has inspired me ever since. In fact, one of his favorite phrases he shared with me has become a guiding compass of sorts: *Make each day your masterpiece.* I have taped this to my bathroom mirror, hung it above my computer, and even have it on my cell phone screen.

"It can seem daunting to face a long-term goal – be it graduating from college or earning a masters degree or getting a promotion at work or writing a novel. Or maybe your goal is to run a marathon or climb eleven miles to the summit of Mt. Whitney.

"Whatever your goal is, if you take it one step at a time; if you concentrate on the next one-hundred meters of the hiking trail; the next twenty yards of a race; writing the next page of a term paper or novel; if you focus on making each day your masterpiece – specifically, making *today* your masterpiece – well then it becomes doable. And it also becomes more enjoyable."

And, of course, it is always enjoyable to help others with their own masterpieces.

Twenty

Footwork

———

"There is great joy in doing something for somebody else."
– John Wooden,
in a note to Dallas and Greg

Δ

The following essay that Greg wrote during his junior year at the University of Southern California, titled "Thankful for an Experience of a Lifetime," embodies the impact Coach Wooden's life has had on him.

Δ

As I slipped the new pair of running shoes onto my host's calloused feet, adrenaline surged through my body like at the starting line of a race. Even though I had anticipated and imagined this scene many times over, I was still overcome by the unbridled joy of giving these shoes to the dignified elder Chief of Sikoro, a tiny and impoverished village in Mali, West Africa. My hands trembled. My heartbeat raced.

The scene unfolded a few days after Christmas 2009. I had traveled to Sikoro along with eleven fellow University of Southern California students on a three-week humanitarian trip through the USC Africa Health Initiative. Our mission included building an irrigated community garden to enrich the 500 villagers' diets with fruits and vegetables as well as donating funds we raised to purchase building materials for a desperately needed bridge. During the rainy season, the nearby river floods, leaving Sikoro isolated from nearly all schools, commerce and, often tragically, medical services.

I brought along 113 pairs of running shoes – as many as I could squeeze into five extra duffle bags – to give out to the villagers.

Three years previously, when I was a student at Ventura High School, I founded Give Running to collect, clean, and donate new and used running shoes to disadvantaged youth. To be honest, I am humbled that my original holiday project with a modest goal of 100 pairs of shoes has snowballed into an official 501(c)(3) nonprofit organization that has given more than 14,000 pairs of running and athletic shoes to underprivileged kids near and far, from inner-city Los Angeles to indigent villages and orphanages in developing nations including Kenya,

Liberia, Uganda, Sudan, and more recently earthquake victims in Haiti.

Sikoro, however, was the first time outside of California that I was able to carry out our motto in person: *"Give opportunity. Give joy. Give Running."* As is often the case when one gives, I found I received so much more in return. I am so thankful for the opportunity I had to visit Sikoro. Indeed, as the great coach and humanitarian John Wooden once wisely told me when I was blessed to meet him a few years ago: "There is great joy in doing something for somebody else."

Mali ranks as the third-poorest nation in the world, and yet to me it seemed like its people must rank among the happiest on the planet. To an outsider from the West, this is at first surprising if not downright perplexing. After all, the villagers in Sikoro live in mud-brick huts; sleep on woven mats on hard dirt floors; and pump their water – *ji* in Bambara, their native language – from two wells. And, as mentioned, they lack enough fruits and vegetables, lack adequate medical care, lack year-round schooling.

While living with difficult challenges, they are clearly happy: smiling constantly, laughing easily, dancing freely. Worries about car payments and mortgages and pension accounts and work promotions do not weigh on their minds. They don't have much materially by our standards, but they have enough – and most importantly, what they have they graciously share. *Dumuni* (food), especially *sogo* (meat), is in short supply yet the villagers slaughtered a *ba* (goat) to treat us to a celebratory feast.

In return I could not wait to *djan* (give) them the gift of running shoes. Unfortunately, our USCAHI group's luggage was lost on our connecting flight from Paris. Over the next week the rest of our group's luggage trickled in . . . but not mine. For two weeks I made do with the clothes on my back, an inconvenience that would have been infuriating had I not taken to heart Coach John Wooden's sagacity: "Things turn out best for those who make the best of the way things turn out."

Indeed, I embraced the turn of events as it allowed me to more fully relate to, and appreciate, the people of Sikoro. For a brief while, I was living with about the same few personal possessions as did they. Still, I was worried heartsick that the five duffle bags filled with gift footwear would not be found.

At long last the duffle bags arrived and my dream of handing out the running shoes was realized. Recalling it still gives me goose bumps. For many of the Sikoro villagers, these were the first footwear they ever had. Indeed, so precious were the shoes that if we at first guessed wrong and gave a person shoes that were a half-size – or even more – too small, our recipient would crunch up his or her toes and insist the shoes fit just fine! Painfully too small was better than none at all; we could not take the shoes off the person's feet until we brought over a larger replacement pair.

As special as was honoring the Chief with the first pair of running shoes, lacing up each pair on the other recipients' feet was equally touching. However, one gift pair stands out in my mind and heart as distinctly as does the greatest run of my life.

The day before leaving Sikoro, I went on a six-mile run through the village. The first several laps of my quarter-mile loop I ran in solitude, but then several children began to run with me. They would keep me company for one or two circuits, then drop out to rest, only to rejoin me the next time I came around. Before I knew it, my running group had swelled from three to ten to twenty-plus smiling kids – many of whom were wearing the gift shoes they had recently received.

During this most memorable run of my life, one training partner stood out because he had to stop – not out of exhaustion, but because he was running barefoot and we had reached a rocky section on the trail. Lameen Sacko, I learned, had not received a pair of Give Running shoes the day before. The following day, my last in the village, I met Lameen at his mud hut and asked him to try on my personal running shoes – the only pair of footwear (besides flip-flops) I had brought for my own use in Mali.

My size-11½ Adidas SuperNova Glides fit Lameen perfectly. "*I ni che, Amadou* (Thank you, Greg)," he said, using my adopted Malian name.

"*I ni su* (You're welcome)," I relied, smiling.

As we shook hands in friendship, adrenaline again surged through my body and my heartbeat again raced. I realized how each pair of Give Running gift shoes serves as a bridge between two people. While the giver and receiver of each pair of footwear may not meet face-to-face as did Lameen and I, through the shoes they nevertheless meet "foot-to-foot" and heart-to-heart.

Visiting Africa, I found, breaks your heart – and opens it wider than before. I am certainly a better and more fulfilled person for the experience.

This Thanksgiving when I sit down to a feast of turkey, I will think of the special *ba* dinner I was treated to in Sikoro. I will give thanks for all I have, and all I learned from those half a world away. I will also think of Lameen when I lace up my new Adidas to go for a run.

Δ

One of my favorite photographs from Greg's trip to Mali shows him kneeling down and, like a parent helping a small child, putting a brand-new running sock onto a calloused foot of Sikoro's Elder Chief before next lacing up the pair of gift running shoes for the esteemed host. The image warms my proud heart because it reminds me of photos I have seen of Mother Teresa washing the bare feet of villagers; too, I image Greg taking great care to smooth out the wrinkles in the socks of the Elder Chief just as Coach Wooden showed Greg during their shared visit years earlier in Coach's home.

Greg visited Africa again – Ghana this time – in January of 2012. He brought along more shoes and also led his first "Pyramid Running Camps" for more than three hundred youth in which he emphasized many of the lessons from the Pyramid of Success.

Below is a blog article Greg wrote for *The Huffington Post* about that second trip to West Africa – and about some of the wisdom he learned from Coach Wooden, who once said: "Time lost is time lost. It's gone forever. Some people tell themselves that they will work twice as hard tomorrow to make up for what they did not do today. People should always do their best. If they work twice as hard tomorrow, then they should have also worked twice as hard today. That would have been their best."

Δ

There is something mystical about the moment of selecting a fortune cookie. The anticipation is often more thrilling to me than actually cracking open the cookie itself.

The dinner table inevitably goes silent when four sugary mysteries are dealt out to four pairs of waiting, wondering hands. Even when I'm making a quick stop at Panda Express on my way to Painting class, I feel my hand's slight hesitation over the fortune cookie bowl as I try to intuit the right choice – or is it that I want the right fortune cookie to sense and select me?

Of all the fortunes I have received, my favorite was one of those Painting class Panda Express slips of paper. The message read: *Counting time is not so important as making time count.*

Being a competitive distance runner and four-year member of the USC Track & Field Team, this wisdom immediately resonated with my deep passion for running and the deepest reasons why I train and race. The ultimate triumph of running is not in *counting time* – in the race results and personal records that can be measured against runners past, present, and future. Rather, running's true greatness sources from *making time count* – because above all, running is a practice for living well. Self-understanding and camaraderie with teammates form the real fortune.

My time in Ghana, West Africa this past winter reaffirmed my fortune cookie's truth. I led Give Running's team on a ten-day trip to Ghana to hold our first international Pyramid Running Camp. In addition to teaching kids proper running technique, well-balanced training, nutrition, sports psychology, and injury prevention, we also worked on leadership, teamwork, goal-setting, and achieving personal success by giving one's best effort.

With Coach John Wooden being one of my most esteemed role models whom I once had the privilege to spend an afternoon visiting with in his home, my favorite exercise challenged teams of youth campers to find and then assemble different character trait blocks to physically build Coach Wooden's Pyramid of Success – thus the name "Pyramid Running Camp."

We also partnered with the two local NGOs iStandAbove and Witness Hope to conduct a soccer tournament, coaching clinic, and basketball clinic. In total, we worked with more than three-hundred youth and twenty-five elite coaches, using sports to engage the community in how the lessons and character traits forged through sports apply to all aspects of life. Other highlights from the humanitarian trip included donating Give Running shoes; distributing food to hundreds of disadvantaged children in one of the most impoverished neighborhoods in Accra, Ghana's capital city; and being interviewed live on Ghanaian national television.

My experiences in Ghana taught me that I am my most authentic and joyous self when I am empowering others to run forward: toward dreams, toward passions, toward fulfilling lives. Making others count makes time count.

"A long life may not be good enough," Ben Franklin wisely noted, "but a good life is long enough." It is not the time that we count, but rather the time that we *make* count which matters most. Unless we make time count, after all, does measuring it even matter? This holds true far beyond the realm of running.

Life is fragile. The poverty I witnessed in Ghana broke my heart. The horrific 2013 Boston Marathon bombing is but our most recent reminder that living a long life is beyond our control.

But life is also beautiful. Even in a time of deep suffering, the goodwill and kind deeds around us each day are a constant reminder that leading a good life is a gift we can choose to share with the world. As we grieve for lost loved ones and work to correct injustice, may we remember that giving is good medicine.

Indeed, individuals and whole communities are coming together to make sense of death by fully embracing life: some donate blood to save the lives of strangers, others contribute to funds supporting victims. The connections we forge and the joy we kindle helps us heal. We move beyond counting time, and mourning lost time, in order to make time count by helping others as best we can.

Too often, it takes a shooting or a journey halfway around the world to remind us to not take any moment for granted – as well as to remind us how much a single moment can matter.

The hands of the clock can measure a long life, but only our own hands can make it good.

Twenty-One

A Kindness (Finally) Repaid

———

*"You can't live a perfect day without doing something for
someone who will never be able to repay you."*

– John Wooden

Δ

I happily shared an experience with Coach about a time
many years ago when someone else lived a perfect day by
doing something nice for me and my young family. In
September 2010 I finally repaid that debt, embarrassingly
far too many years belatedly – and three months too late to
share the follow-up kindness with Coach, who had passed
away the previous June.

Perhaps what is more important, however, is that
the original experience is one that Lisa and I talked about
with Dallas and Greg when it occurred, and numerous
times in the years since, as being an example of Coach
Wooden's ideal of helping others without thought of
receiving anything in return. That is, receiving anything

other than contentment and pride in living a more perfect day because of it.

Δ

The first night of our honeymoon in Las Vegas – where the wedding did not take place, by the way – my beautiful bride and I dined at a charming Italian restaurant named "Battista's Hole In The Wall." It was a meal to forever fondly remember. When the restaurant's elderly accordion player Gordy came tableside and learned we were from Ventura in Southern California, he played and campily sang "California Here I Come."

Fifteen years later we returned to Battista's, this time with our then eleven-year-old daughter and eight-year-old son. Again Gordy performed "California Here I Come." Again the meal was wonderful – surely Mike Tyson, whose fight I had come to cover as a sports columnist, would have found the meatballs tastier than Evander Holyfield's ear.

We were enjoying ourselves, in no hurry to leave, but after a while Dallas and Greg grew impatient as we waited for the check. Ten minutes became twenty and then a full thirty and now Lisa and I too were impatient.

"Where's the check?" I grumbled.

"Where's our waiter?" Lisa echoed.

"Where's the bathroom?" the restless kids needed to know.

Gordy came by a second time, but still our waiter remained AWOL. Eventually, finally, at long last I caught the attention of a different waiter. I asked if he could get our check. He disappeared.

We left without paying.

Before you get a totally wrong idea, let me explain.

Our waiter finally returned and proceeded to tell us that the two gentlemen at a table across the room had paid for our dinner, but requested he not let us know until after they were gone. They saw a happy young family, the waiter explained, and simply wanted to do something nice without us having to thank them.

Wow. Those two men gave us far more than an expensive meal free of charge – they gave the four of us a warm memory we talk about to this day. More importantly, those two gentlemen gave us a life lesson in random acts of kindness and the lasting power of giving. Coffee and a sandwich for a homeless person; texting a donation to an earthquake or hurricane relief fund; new backpacks, school supplies, books or running shoes for kids in need – Dallas and Greg recall that long-ago Las Vegas dinner as part of their motivation to routinely do all of the above.

Lisa and I feel similarly. Still, while the Hole In The Wall dinner bill has been "paid forward" in full many times over the years, I always felt that the particular kind act itself had not been squared; a proper and worthy and specific "thank you" not given.

Thirteen years passed since that special summer evening. That is a long time. Too long, by far. For a stretch I had kept my eyes out for the perfect occasion to anonymously say, "Put their dinner on my MasterCard," but eventually I guess I just stopped looking. With Coach's death I was reminded of my long-overdue dinner debt; I began looking anew for an opportune restaurant scene worthy of portrayal by Norman Rockwell.

One evening shortly thereafter as I was waiting at the front counter for my take-out order to be readied at a local steakhouse, a U.S. soldier dressed in desert camouflage fatigues walked in. He wore a backpack that looked about three times as heavy as a middle-schooler's, which is saying something these days, yet he effortlessly stood tall and erect. "MORGAN" said a name patch on the back of the pack.

"Hi," I said. "I want to thank you for all you do."

"I appreciate that very much, Sir," the authentic American hero humbly replied, smiling warmly as we shook hands. I imagined my dad and Coach Wooden, who had both served in the Navy during World War II (Wooden, then thirty-one, enlisted shortly after Pearl Harbor and my dad was drafted on his eighteenth birthday in November

1944), once looking so young and so brave and so strong, and I thought about the unrepayable debts I owed them.

Too, my mind went back to the poem "Two Sides of War" by Grantland Rice. Coach recited it to me on our very first walk together:

Two Sides of War

All wars are planned by older men
In council rooms apart,
Who call for greater armament
And map the battle chart.

But out along the shattered field
Where golden dreams turn gray,
How very young the faces were
Where all the dead men lay.

Portly and solemn in their pride,
The elders cast their vote
For this or that, or something else,
• *That sounds the martial note.*

But where their sightless eyes stare out
Beyond life's vanished toys,
I've noticed nearly all the dead
Were hardly more than boys.

I wanted to say more than "thank you for all you do," something less trite, but a table for two was ready and the hostess led the strapping soldier and his visibly proud mother away. As I watched them walk off and be seated it struck me that, as in Rice's famous poem, the soldier was hardly more than a boy. Probably older than Greg, then twenty, but younger than Dallas, twenty-three at the time; his mother about Lisa's and my age.

I hope they ordered an appetizer *each*, beer and wine, soup *and* salad, and prime rib entrees so big even a hungry serviceman had his work cut out cleaning his plate, plus dessert and coffee.

And afterwards I hope the family of two had to wait a while, enjoying each other's company and some laughs even as they grew a little bit impatient wondering where in the world their waiter was with the check.

Twenty-Two

Friendliness

———

*"If we magnified blessings as much as we magnify
disappointments, we would all be much happier."*

— John Wooden

Δ

When I am running it is my nature to smile and give a
"runner's nod" or quick wave to others I encounter on the
roads, trails and bike paths. In more intimate social
situations, as with many writers, I am a bit introverted.
However, Coach Wooden helped me become more
outgoing with a folksy story from his life. It remains one of
my favorites.

Δ

On the way to the airport after a weeklong stay in Southern
California, the visitor from the Midwest complained to his
transplanted host: "John, I honestly don't know how you

can stand to live here. No one is friendly here like they are back home."

"Sure they are," the host answered. "What do you mean?"

"I mean I've been here an entire week and not a single person out on the street or sidewalks has said 'Hi' to me."

"Did you say 'Hello' to them?" asked the host.

"Well, no, because I didn't know any of them."

John Wooden, the host for his visiting Hoosier friend, shared this anecdote – this life lesson – with me more than a couple times. Each retelling was punctuated by a wry smile.

I was reminded of this story when I traveled to West Lafayette, Indiana to visit Dallas at Purdue University, Wooden's alma mater, which is only ninety miles from Coach's hometown of Martinsville. For good reason Purdue proudly claims "Johnny" as its favorite son to this day.

Back to Wooden's story about the visitor and friendliness. I would like to share a few scenes that played out during my small-town Indiana trip.

At the airport, from across a large room an elderly woman asked the airline workers if they had someone who could help with her luggage. When no response came, she asked again, more loudly, and in more distress. This time an airline worker yelled back, his voice cold and uncaring: "No, ma'am!"

In a blink, a traveler in the middle of a long line gave up his place to go assist the woman. The friendliness did not end there. When the Good Samaritan returned to the *end* of the line, the person at the very front beckoned him to go before her – which, incidentally, was much further ahead than where he had been standing before he went to help. What is more, the rest of the people in line warmly waved him forward.

Also I saw this: A mother in a parking lot with a small child balanced on one hip, a bag of groceries in the other arm and car keys apparently misplaced in her purse. In stepped another woman who kindly lent a helping hand and also took her shopping cart to the return rack.

Another example: A gentleman in a suit and tie raced out of a bagel shop for about one hundred yards in pursuit of a young woman pushing a stroller in order to give her the pacifier her baby had dropped.

And another: A boy, no older than eight, was a quarter short paying for a smoothie and began searching his pockets for more change. A stranger behind him, college-aged, reached into his own pocket and handed the needed coin to the cashier. A small thing, yes, but it mattered to the young boy.

Lastly: Hellos from strangers; friendly smiles in passing; small talk and small acts of kindness. There is nothing like Hoosier hospitality – except that all of the above travel-day scenes happened in Ventura and Los Angeles International Airport *before* I arrived in Indiana.

As Civil War Union General Joshua Chamberlain observes in Michael Shara's Pulitzer Prize-winning novel *The Killer Angels*: "Home. One place is like another, really. Maybe not. But the truth is it's all just rock and dirt and people are roughly the same."

Coach Wooden knew this well. Sometimes you just have to say "Hello" first.

Twenty-Three

Teamwork

———

*"It is amazing how much can be accomplished if no one
cares who gets the credit."*

— John Wooden

Δ

One of my favorite teamwork maxims by Coach Wooden is,
"It takes ten hands to put the ball in the basket." While he
was obviously speaking specifically about basketball with
five players on the court trying to score, it is a wonderful
metaphor for all pursuits. It also brings to mind the Kenyan
term *harambee*, which translates to "all pull together."
Harambee is an august tradition where the community
works as a whole to help itself; indeed, Kenyans are taught,
much like Coach Wooden's players were, that no person
can achieve very much without the support of those around
him or her.

To put this idea into further perspective, Coach
recited a poem by Saxon White Kessinger that was also a

favorite of his longtime UCLA athletic trainer Ducky Drake.

The Indispensible Man

Sometimes when you're feeling important
Sometimes when your ego's in bloom
Sometimes when you think that you are
The best qualified man in the room

Sometimes when you think that your absence
Would leave an unfillable hole
Just follow these simple instructions
And see how they humble your soul

Take a bucket and fill it with water
Put your hand in it up to your wrist
Then take it back out and the hole that remains
Is the measure of how you'll be missed

Now you can splash as much as you want to
You can stir up the water for sure
Then stop and you see in a moment
That the water's the same as before

Now the moral to this is quite simple
You must do the best that you can
But you'll always be wise to remember
There is no indispensible man

One time when Coach was talking with me about how indispensible teamwork and selflessness are, I shared with him a story that pleased him greatly. It happened in a small farm town in Ohio where a young girl had wandered away from home. She became lost in the family's wheat field that had grown taller than she was. Her family called out her name and searched frantically, but could not find her.

Soon neighbors joined the search, but as night began to fall the little girl still had not been found. Pretty soon half the townspeople had come to help and were running through the wheat field trying to find the little girl, but with no success. The field was simply too big.

Night fell, and with it the temperature. If the little girl was not found soon, she would surely die from the bitter cold. Finally, the little girl's father called everyone in from the wheat field.

No, he was not giving up on finding his dear daughter.

Rather, he had an idea. He gathered all the volunteers together and had them join hands to form a long human chain. More accurately, they formed a "human comb." Then they walked together, side by side by side, and combed through the tall, amber waves of grain. This way they did not miss a single area as they had been doing when they searched separately as individuals.

Within ten minutes, the search party of nearly one hundred individuals now united as one found the little girl curled up on the ground – shivering and trying to stay warm, but still alive.

In a larger sense, the wheat field is the world; we are all lost at times and need others to help us overcome our own "wheat field challenges." Other times we must offer the helping hand. Certainly I was very blessed to have Coach figuratively take my hand in his for nearly a quarter century.

When I finished telling the tale, Coach smiled and said it pleased him very much. Then he shared a similar story with a similar lesson.

It was a beautiful Southern California morning following a stormy night, and a beachcomber was walking along the sand now littered with kelp and driftwood. Off in the distance, he noticed a man who bent down to pick something up and then tossed it into the ocean.

Every few steps, the man repeated this calisthenic: bend, stand, toss. But what was he throwing, the beachcomber wondered: Driftwood sticks? Skipping stones?

As the two morning walkers neared each other, the beachcomber finally realized the man was picking up starfish that, by the hundreds, had been washed ashore by the storm's high surf and left stranded on the sand.

The beachcomber could not help but laugh at the other man's futile efforts. "You're just wasting your time," he called out. "There are far too many starfish for you to make a difference before they die."

"Maybe," the other man said as he gently picked up another starfish. "But to this one, I am making a world of difference." And with that, he safely tossed that starfish back into the waves.

Naturally I told this story numerous times to Dallas and Greg when they were growing up, and in his Commencement Speech at USC's Student-Athlete Graduation Ceremony in 2012, Greg shared the wheat field and starfish stories. He also added this beautiful sentiment:

"Growing up, that is where the starfish story always left off, and I don't know what happened next – but I will tell you what I like to think. I think the beachcomber joined the man in his routine: bend, stand, toss.

"And as the beautiful morning unfolded and more people came to the beach, slowly but steadily the impromptu group of starfish rescuers swelled like the gathering of townspeople in that Ohio wheat field.

"And then I think they all joined hands and together combed the driftwood- and kelp-covered shorefront until – one bend, stand, and toss at a time – they had saved all the starfish on that sunny strand."

As Greg delivered his moving speech I could almost feel Coach Wooden's pleased spirit inside the Galen Center arena. Coach may have been a UCLA Bruin blue-and-through, but he valued education over school colors and was overjoyed when he learned first that Dallas, and three years later Greg, would be attending USC on merit-based Trustee Scholarships.

"I'm proud of you," he told each of them upon hearing the news. "USC is a wonderful school where you will get an excellent education. Study hard, as I know you will, but be sure also to make time for fun."

Making time for joining hands with others is also important.

•

Twenty-Four

Little Brother Steps Up Big

———

"Be at your best when your best is needed."
— John Wooden

Δ

In the Easter morning video the girl, almost six, benevolently leaves the easy-to-see colored eggs for her three-year-old brother to collect. When he has difficulty finding some of them, she guides him with hints and sometimes a pointing finger. In the end, his weaved basket has the bulk of the bounty compared to hers.

In many ways, the scene encapsulates the two decades that have followed: the big sister has always looked out for her little brother, even after he literally became the bigger one at six-foot-three. Indeed, it is often the case even after we become adults that we remain locked in our childhood roles among family.

The last week in March 2013 a crisis struck. Let's just say the bottom fell out of an Easter basket, spilling and breaking the brightly dyed eggs. The girl, Dallas, now a young woman, phoned from twenty-two-hundred miles away at Purdue University where she was in the final semester of earning her MFA in Fiction Writing.

"Distraught" falls far shy in describing her emotional state after breaking off her engagement to be married the following year. It is times like this that a daughter needs her mother. However, because Lisa was being squeezed in a deadline vise at her work, Dallas insisted she could manage and that Mom stay home.

Similarly, Dallas insisted that I also stay put to continue helping care for my own father – her beloved "Gramps" – who had just undergone knee replacement surgery. Briefly, the roles had been turned upside-down as the grown son became the father and the father became the son.

And younger brother Greg surely could not fly out to be by her side because he was physically and mentally exhausted, having just arrived home the night before the crisis struck after travelling for twenty hours across twelve time zones following a five-week humanitarian sojourn halfway around the globe in Sri Lanka.

While Lisa and I discussed matters, Greg went online at ten p.m. and booked himself a flight, the last-minute ransom pricing causing him no pause. "She needs me," he said simply, emphatically, as he hurriedly packed.

In bed at midnight, he rose at three a.m. to make his crack-of-dawn flight. Upon landing three time zones east he took a long bus ride and then a short taxi trip to her doorstep a little after six p.m.

To this sentimental fool it brought to mind the closing scene in "It's A Wonderful Life." Harry, a Navy pilot and war hero, leaves in the middle of a banquet where President Truman is presenting him with the Congressional Medal of Honor to fly through a blizzard from New York City to Bedford Falls because his big brother George is in a crisis.

Despite the three-years age difference, it is not rare for people being introduced to Dallas and Greg to inquire if they are twins. Beyond appearance, they have always shared a twin-like bond. But perhaps never were they closer than during this tribulation.

"He's the best gift you and Mom ever gave me," Dallas said on the phone the night Greg arrived.

Over the next seven days, he proved to be penicillin for the ailment. He employed every block in the Pyramid of Success, put countless Wooden-isms into action, and called upon the lesson of the "Self-Esteem Ape." He walked Dallas to and from classes; made sure she was eating enough; watched a marathon of chick flicks with her. In short, Greg was at his best when his best was needed. He tackled the crisis head-on and provided leadership and labor, poise and protection, wisdom and support, loving words and a shoulder to cry on, all on his own, all on little sleep.

Sometimes the son becomes the father; certainly my young man became a man, period. Or, as Dallas noted: "I have always been the big sister, but this week Greg has become my big brother."

Asked how he was holding up midway through his rescue mission, Greg quoted former Navy Seal Eric Greitens, who wrote in his best-selling book *The Heart and the Fist*: "When a task is necessary, its difficulty is irrelevant."

When his sister needed help, everything else was irrelevant.

"She's the best gift you ever gave me," the younger brother continued, echoing what his big sis had said of him days earlier – words that are the best gift a parent could ever hear.

And so in many ways, like a favorite old Easter morning video, I cherish the crisis that has now passed.

Twenty-Five

A Final Farewell

———

*"May His love and that of those near and dear to you
bring solace and hope in this time of need."*

– John Wooden,

in a condolence letter to my dad

Δ

I am beyond blessed to have known John Wooden, who as a man far surpassed his legend. For twenty-three years he made my life – and Lisa, Dallas and Greg's lives – better and richer and more *successful* according to Coach's definition.

The morning following his death I pulled out the letters Coach sent me. They came first with twenty-two-cent stamps, then stamps of twenty-five cents, twenty-nine cents, thirty-two cents, thirty-nine cents, forty-two cents and Forever Stamps – all of them priceless to me, their memories indeed forever. Letters reminding me to "Make each day your masterpiece" and "Be quick, but don't hurry."

Letters.

October 6, 1987: *"Many thanks for the kind words and your thoughtfulness.*

"Dallas Nicole must be a real joy to you and her mother and it is good to learn that she is doing so well...."

March 10, 1988: *"Dallas is truly something to behold – happy and beautiful. You are blessed...."*

April 7, 1989: *"The article on Jamaal Wilkes, one of my very favorites, was very enjoyable as were the photos of that beautiful bright-eyed Dallas Nicole!*

"Many thanks for sharing.

"If you should call me there should be no problem in getting together for an early morning walk...."

February 9, 1990: *"Congratulations to you on your promotion to lead full-time columnist for the Ventura Star-Free press and special congratulations to your entire family on the arrival of Gregory Ansel Woodburn.*

"If all goes well, I will become a great-grandparent for the third time on this coming May 1...."

November 6, 1992: *"Your column regarding your mother was very beautiful and touching. My sympathy reaches out to all those near and dear to her. I have sent a note to your father and enclosed a few things that had been of some help to me after Nellie's death...."*

March 31, 1994: *"Many thanks for your continued interest and for your article on Keith Wilkes. He belongs in the Hall of Fame! Happy Easter!..."*

December 22, 1995: *"Dear Woody and Family –*

"Of course, it is quite normal, but it is almost impossible to believe how quickly the little ones grow up. They are beautiful.

"I hope the holiday season is good to all of you and the new year will be the same and bring all nations in this troubled world nearer enduring peace and all people closer to true love for one another...."

July 15, 1995: *"I enjoyed your article on Dallas as I have others you have written. They do grow up in a hurry. I see it in my nine great-grandchildren, the oldest will be 10 on Sept. 6 and the youngest came along last Easter Sunday. They have been my salvation since losing my dear Nellie over ten years ago.*

"My son had triple by-pass surgery Wednesday along with carotid artery surgery and is having some problems.

"I am off to the hospital where I have been for the last few days and will be for some time to come...."

August 22, 1997 (after I sent him another book of poetry in thanks for the memory-of-a-lifetime visit with Dallas and Greg, who wrote Coach separate thank-you letters): *"There is great joy in learning that someone feels that something you have said or done has been meaningful to another – especially when it was done without thought of something of material value in return. Thanks!..."*

Also August 22, 1997: *"Dear Dallas and Greggie –*

"Many thanks for your letter.

"Your words of commendation were very kind and deeply appreciated. It was very nice of you to take the time to express yourselves.

"I, too, enjoyed our visit and hope to see you again. Please remember that, as the new school year is here, to work hard on your studies, but keep some time for play.

"Love, John Wooden"

That is a sampling and so on they go, though there is not a letter from Coach in 2010. In my last note to him sent in early May 2010, I shared news that Dallas would be attending graduate school at his alma mater, Purdue, beginning that upcoming fall. I knew Coach would be tickled – and would probably tease me that this makes up for her and Greg going to USC instead of UCLA. When no reply came, I grew worried; Coach's health had been failing in recent years. In 2009, he battled through pneumonia – which my Grandpa Ansel called "The Old Man's Friend" because it often provided a suffering elderly patient with a painless passing. The year prior Coach had been hospitalized briefly after breaking his collarbone and left wrist in a fall at home.

When I learned that Coach was once again in the UCLA Medical Center, my fears worsened. I thought back to how he had held a nearly uninterrupted vigil at Nell's bedside in the hospital – and now a worldwide family was holding an emotional vigil for his recovery.

On Friday, June 4, I got an evening phone call at home from an editor at my newspaper with dreaded news: John Wooden had passed away. He was ninety-nine years old: in four months and ten days he would have completed his one-hundredth trip around the sun.

My initial reaction was, of course, great grief and its close kin tears. In short time, however, I found solace in my memories. Too, I realized that by being so open about his faith, Coach had once again given a gift to the rest of us. His inner peace with his own death, whenever it should arrive, and his unshakable belief that he would then be reunited with his dearly beloved Nell was a potent salve for our earthly heartbreak.

Δ

The moment I hung up the phone with my editor asking me to write a column, even before sharing the mournful news with Lisa and Dallas and Greg, I walked through our home looking at photographs of Coach with me; of Coach with Dallas and Greg.

I also paused at other mementos that reminded me of Coach: the framed Pyramid of Success embossed print that Greg made in an art class that hangs in a place of honor in our family room; the signed Seven-Point Creed in a thick acrylic block on my dresser; the Gartlan limited-edition John Wooden figurine in my bedroom bookcase; the new leather basketball my wife asked Coach to autograph for me because I simply could never infringe on our relationship by doing so myself.

The parade of memories continued to march across my mind's eye as I moved my mourning upstairs: the special Pyramids of Success in Dallas' and Greg's bedrooms given to them upon the happy occasions of their births; and the framed UCLA jerseys signed to both of them "With Love."

Next I paused at the bookcase in my study to look at my old Player's Notebook and the autographed books Coach gave me: *They Call Me Coach* and *Be Quick – But Don't Hurry* and *Wooden: A Lifetime of Observations and Reflections on and Off the Court* and *Wooden on Leadership: How to Create a Winning Organization.*

On the same shelf is another of his small-gesture gifts, an encased Fellowship of Christian Athletes trading card of Coach John Wooden that notes, and perfectly it seems to me, that his favorite scripture is 1 Corinthians 13:

> Though I speak with the tongues of men and of angels, but have not love, I have become sounding brass or a clanging cymbal. And though I have *the gift of*

prophecy, and understand all mysteries and all knowledge, and though I have all faith, so that I could remove mountains, but have not love, I am nothing. And though I bestow all my goods to feed *the poor,* and though I give my body to be burned, but have not love, it profits me nothing.

Love suffers long *and* is kind; love does not envy; love does not parade itself, is not puffed up; does not behave rudely, does not seek its own, is not provoked, thinks no evil; does not rejoice in iniquity, but rejoices in the truth; bears all things, believes all things, hopes all things, endures all things.

Love never fails. But whether *there are* prophecies, they will fail; whether *there are* tongues, they will cease; whether *there is* knowledge, it will vanish away. For we know in part and we prophesy in part. But when that which is perfect has come, then that which is in part will be done away.

When I was a child, I spoke as a child, I understood as a child, I thought as a child; but when I became a man, I put away childish things. For now we see in a mirror, dimly, but then face to face. Now I know in part, but then I shall know just as I also am known.

And now abide faith, hope, love, these three; but the greatest of these *is* love.

Also in the bookcase along with this religious trading card emphasizing the importance Coach placed on the word *love* is a framed black-and-white photograph of Johnny Wooden in his physical prime, in 1932, in his *PURDUE* basketball jersey when he was the indefatigable "Indiana Rubber Man."

And on a nearby wall where I can see them if I look up from my writing desk are two more Pyramids of Success – my first one from the 1975 John Wooden Basketball Fundamentals Camp and a newer, fancier one given to me as a birthday gift a dozen years ago.

Also hanging on display is a black-and-white poster Coach gave me early in our friendship titled "John Wooden On Staying Power" that features a picture of him posed in front of a blackboard used to diagram two basketball plays. The framed poster includes many Wooden-isms: "I believe for every artificial peak you create, you also create valleys . . . There's no pillow as soft as a clear conscious . . . Why do so many people dread adversity, when it is only through adversity that we grow stronger? . . . Your character is what you really are, your reputation is only what others think you are."

While in my study, I opened a small fireproof safe and took out the short stack of cherished letters from Coach; when I reread them in full the following day my mind relived almost every memory contained in the pages of this book. Sitting there, studying a photograph of Coach and me, I recalled a special trait about him – a trait F. Scott Fitzgerald perhaps best articulates in this passage from his literary pyramid, *The Great Gatsby*:

> He smiled understandingly – much more than understandingly. It was one of those rare smiles with a quality of eternal reassurance in it, that you may come across four or five times in life. It faced – or seemed to face – the whole eternal world for an instant, and then concentrated on *you* with an irresistible prejudice in your favor. It understood you just as far as you wanted to be understood, believed in you as you would believe in yourself, and assured you that it had precisely the impression of you that, at your best, you hoped to convey.

When I look back, that is how Coach made me feel from our very first morning walk together.

There is a headstone in Ireland, from where my ancestors originally emigrated to America nearly two and a half centuries ago, that bears this epitaph: "And to my deceased father – Death leaves a heartache no one can heal, love leaves a memory no one can steal."

This is how I feel about Coach Wooden. His friendship, his lessons, his love and spirit in my heart cannot be stolen. Daily, Coach comes to mind – my runner's ID dog tag includes the quote "Make Each Day Your Masterpiece"; I use acronyms of his sayings as computer passwords; I text his Wooden-isms to Dallas and Greg and Lisa; and on it goes.

Upstairs in my study on the night of his passing, eyes still teary some thirty minutes after learning that Coach – like his hero Abraham Lincoln – now belonged to the ages, another emotional wave washed over me. As when I followed the ambulance taking preemie Dallas to the airport on her way to a distant NICU, I once again spoke aloud softly in prayer. This time I repeated some favored words I long ago memorized from the first letter Coach ever sent me: "Although it is often used without true feeling, when it is used with sincerity, no collection of words can be more expressive or meaningful than the very simple word – Thanks!" To which I bowed my head and added: "For your friendship and mentorship and love, Coach – Thanks!"

On the wall rising along the staircase in our home are twenty-three portraits, one taken annually at Christmastime, of Dallas and Greg posing together beginning when Greg was one year old. In each picture they have a different prop or theme, such as wearing their pajamas and clutching Mickey Mouse and Winnie-the-Pooh stuffed toys when they were Little Ones; each wearing their

Cougars letterman jackets the lone year they were at Ventura High School together; and jointly holding a beautiful hand-carved wooden African mask after Greg returned from his humanitarian trip to Mali.

This Wall of Memories includes the portrait taken in December 2010, six months after Coach passed away: Greg is wearing a mourning-black shirt and Dallas is similarly dressed in a black Purdue T-shirt, and together they are holding a framed Pyramid of Success.

My two Little Ones, not even born when Coach entered my life, are now nearly as old as I was when I first walked with him. Despite the sorrow it marks, this picture warms my heart because it also consecrates the important role Coach had – and will continue to have – in our family.

Indeed, far dearer than our photographs with Coach Wooden, and the letters he wrote and the material gifts of signed books and jerseys and basketballs he gave us, are the enduring memories he left us with and the fine friendship and love he showed us.

And, most surely, the life lessons he taught us, through words certainly and through deed and example always: *Success is peace of mind which is a direct result of self-satisfaction in knowing you did your best to become the best you are capable of becoming.*

Be quick, but don't hurry. There is great joy in doing something for somebody else. Make friendship a fine art.

Happiness begins where selfishness ends. Good things take time, usually a lot of time. Work hard on your studies, but keep some time for play. Love is nothing unless we give it to someone.

Above all, *Make Each Day Your Masterpiece.*

Acknowledgements

———

"It takes ten hands to put the ball in the basket," Coach told me, but putting *Wooden & Me* into print took many dozen. To point an acknowledging finger to each individual who has selflessly assisted me on this long, winding, wonderful journey from conception to manuscript to publication would be impossible.

And yet, at the risk of leaving out many who merit mention, I wish to specifically offer my thanks to a few – beginning with my two remarkable adult children, Dallas and Greg, who have turned the tables on me as a parent by becoming *my* role-models. Dallas and Greg each had a deft hand in this project every step along the way; from living much of this story with me to reading my original manuscript and offering invaluable insights for improvement; from proofreading the final manuscript to orchestrating my Kickstarter fundraising campaign for publication; from encouraging me to celebrating our ultimate shared success. This undertaking has been more consuming than I could have imagined, and yet with Dallas and Greg by my side it has been one of the most enjoyable things I have ever done. Similarly, this book would have been impossible without my college sweetheart-turned-wife Lisa's unconditional love and unwavering support. Also, thanks to my "brother" Frank Paschal for being an inspiration for how to face a long and daunting challenge head-on, day by day and small step by small step, until the ultimate goal has been reached.

I am deeply indebted to my great friend Keven Baxter for countless reasons, including his casual-but-sincere suggestion many years ago that I write a memoir about my friendship with Coach. Thanks additionally to Ken McAlpine, a gifted writer who was my third manuscript reader, for offering his judicious eye and, more importantly, for offering his friendship and belief in me.

One of the most rewarding aspects of this project has been the friends – both old (reaching all the way back to elementary school) and new – who enthusiastically stepped forward to help me. They include, for a rainbow of reasons, and in alphabetical order with apologies to the deserving I have inadvertently left out: Elaine Aldrete, Lynne Andujar, Nestor Aparicio, Howard Beck, Ann Brennan, Dianna Chrysler, Mike Comeaux, Mike Craft, Jeffrey Dransfeldt, Jon Gold, Tom Hoffarth, Lynn Johnston, Barry Kibrick, Dave Stancliff, Kristine Leahy, Steve Lee, Rick Limpert,

Arash Markazi, Linda McCoy-Murray and the late Jim Murray for inspiring me to become a writer in the first place and later befriending me, Jeff McElroy, Shannon McGinn, Judy Mick, Gary Miller, Nanette Overly, Mike Pendleton, Rhiannon Potkey, Steve Pratt, Randy Robertson, Kathy Sena, Tom Spence, Alicia Stratton, Tim Tessalone, the late Chuck Thomas, Stephenie Thomas, Steve Thomas, Reinaldo Vela, Bill Wall, Marissa Walsh, Ed Wehan, Peter Yobo, and, of course, each and every person who pledged their support on Kickstarter.

Lastly, my sincere and ongoing gratitude to the Bryan family – Wayne and Kathy, and Bob and Mike – for their unyielding friendship, support and guidance to the Woodburn family – Lisa and me, and Dallas and Greg. In many ways, beginning when I was age twelve, Wayne has been the matching bookend of Coach Wooden in my life; first as my tennis coach and later as a friend and mentor – and always as a role model. Moreover, collectively, the Bryans are a role-model family.

Because of all these "teammates," and many more who have gone unmentioned, *Wooden & Me* has come to life in print. And so I close with the wise words Coach wrote to me at the start of our friendship: "Although it is often used without true feeling, when it is used with sincerity, no collection of words can be more expressive or meaningful than the very simple word – Thanks!"

About the Author

Woody Woodburn has been a sports columnist for more than twenty-five years in Southern California with *The Ventura County Star* and then *The South Bay Daily Breeze* in Torrance. He is now back with *The Star* in Ventura as a general interest essayist. His journalism career has also had stops in Santa Maria, Paso Robles and Twentynine Palms.

National recognition for Woodburn's writing includes First Place for Column Writing by the Associated Press News Executive Council; Column Writing honors by the Associated Press Sports Editors; E.W. Scripps Newspapers "Columnist of the Year" and Copley News Service's "Columnist of the Year"; and the James S. Copley "Ring of Truth" award. In 2003, Woodburn was inducted into the Jim Murray Memorial Foundation's Journalists Hall of Fame. His work has appeared in *The Best American Sports Writing* anthology, *The Sporting News*, and numerous *Chicken Soup For The Soul* anthologies. He also co-authored

Raising Your Child To Be A Champion In Athletics, Arts and Academics (Kensington Publishing/Citadel Press, 2004) with nationally renowned speaker and coach Wayne Bryan.

Woody lives in Ventura, California, with his wife Lisa; the couple has two adult children, daughter Dallas and son Greg. He can be contacted through his website: woodywoodburn.com.

Made in the USA
San Bernardino, CA
23 October 2015